Smart Money Moves

Get on track and stay on track *early in your career* with these tips, hacks and strategies

By:

The Financial Foundations Program Team:

Kyle Wilke, CFP® and Chelsea Hodl, MBA with Steve Juetten, CFP®

FINANCIAL
FOUNDATIONS

Table of Contents

Disclaimers

This book is for general education purposes only. Therefore, the publisher and authors make no representations or warranties with respect to the accuracy or completeness of the contents of this work and disclaim all warranties of fitness for a particular purpose. The ideas, tips, hacks, and strategies contained herein may not be suitable for every situation. If professional assistance is required, the reader should seek the advice of a competent professional person. The fact that an organization, website, author or any other information source is mentioned in the text does not mean that the authors or publisher endorses that information or services or guarantees the accuracy of the information. While every effort has been made to make this book as complete and accurate as possible, there may be mistakes both typographical and in content. Investment results shown in this book are illustrative only. Past performance is not a guarantee of future experience. Investment markets can and will differ from the information provided here.

INTRODUCTION

Why We Wrote This Book

We talk to early career professionals just like you every day and they ask lots of good questions. We decided to gather together all the best advice we give to these clients in one place, so you can learn from what we tell them and use it to your advantage. Using your money wisely is a balancing act between living for today and saving for tomorrow and we want you to make smart money decisions. If we can help you avoid making mistakes early in your career by making **Smart Money Moves** now, it will make it more fun now and set you up for the future.

How We Hope You Use This Book

This book is not meant to be read through like a novel from cover to cover. Think of this as a resource book to turn to when you have a money question. We find that most money questions come up when some life event is about to happen or has happened. For example, money questions come up when you're thinking about buying a car, starting a new job, or having kids.

Or sometimes money questions come up when you're thinking about your future like how to pay off student loan debt, so you can buy a house or even your financial freedom day (aka "retirement"). If you want to just browse through this book, be our guest. That's fine too. Just use this book in a way that helps you take care of your money and make **Smart Money Moves** so you can do more of what you love to do. That's our wish for you.

If You Have Questions

If we've left something out, please send us an email and let us know. You can reach us at **kyle@finpath.com** or **chelsea@finapth.com**. You can always check out our website at **www.takecareofyourmoney.com** too. Finally, please like us on our **Facebook page**. We post useful articles and videos there often.

SMART MONEY MOVES

MONEY BASICS

Money comes to you in exchange for your work. Once your employer pays you, you have two choices of what to do with the money:

1. Spend it
2. Save it

If you want to be smart about your money, you need a plan for both of these options. Otherwise, money just sort of drifts away like dust and you have nothing to show for it.

*

Okay, everyone knows they should save. But did you know why it's *money smart* to start saving **early,** even if it's only a small amount each month? It's the power of compounding. Ben Franklin (you know, the guy with the kite in the rainstorm?) said compounding is the seventh wonder of the world.

Here's an example. Lauren started saving while she worked in high school and college and is 25 years old now. She has accumulated $10,000 and invests it into a SmartMoney Rules simple portfolio that has a return of 6% annually. She makes no more contributions and lets that $10,000 grow for 40 years until she is ready to retire at 65 years old. Now, let's say that Thomas waits to start saving until he is 35 years old. Thomas starts investing $1,000 per year for 30 years and invests it into a portfolio that also has a return of 6%. Thomas will similarly retire when he is 65. Who will have more at the time they are ready to retire, Lauren, who invested $10,000? Or Thomas, who invested $30,000?

After 40 years, Lauren's one-time investment of $10,000 will have grown to $102,857.18. For Thomas, after 30 years of investing $1,000 per year, his yearly investments will have a value of $79,058.19. This is the power of compound interest. Starting investing early is the best way to take advantage of compound interest. Thanks, Ben.

*

Experiences over things -- that's what this article says matters most to young professionals. It's a good read. What are your thoughts?

http://www.forbes.com/sites/ashleystahl/2016/11/15

/how-millennials-spend-their-money-hint-experiences-
trump-possessions/#62f7bda32406

*

Advice to a Relative Early in His Career

Steve Juetten, CFP®, the Principal of our firm, has a nephew who graduated from college two years ago and is working in a job he likes. At a recent family gathering, the nephew asked Steve for some suggestions on what he might consider doing with his money. In brief, here is what Steve told his nephew:

1. Set aside a portion of each paycheck for long-term future needs.
2. Pay off any student loans and avoid debt in the future.
3. Set some short and intermediate life goals.
4. Read a good book or two about money. Steve suggested "I Will Teach You To Be Rich" by Ramit Sethi and "How to Think About Money" by Jonathan Clements.
5. Start an emergency fund and build it up to about a year of living expenses.
6. You're probably going to changes jobs several times in your career; when you change jobs, make sure to keep health insurance.

7. Diversify investments.
8. Create and stick with a money plan.
9. Short, simple and easy to remember

*

Does the idea of tackling your personal finances seem overwhelming? There's a new strategy to help you approach and take charge of your money. This strategy is called **gamification**. Gamification is the idea that personal finance is like a game with different levels that can be mastered.

Having this mindset helps you take control of your personal finances and it gives you the confidence you need in order to tackle each goal. The beginner levels could be things such as paying off debt, or funding an emergency savings account, or getting your estate documents completed. By having smaller goals, or levels, you are more likely to achieve them. When you see the progress, you've made by accomplishing beginner levels, you'll have the confidence to continue on to the more advanced levels, which might include buying a house or saving for retirement, depending on your personal situation.

Gamification also helps by giving you a starting point. Sometimes, the idea of such a big and important topic like personal finance scares people away because they don't know where to start. There are many moving pieces and you might not know where to jump in. So we say, if you use gamification as your strategy to approach your finances, a great starting place is to set up automatic deposits into an online savings account, so that eventually you can level up by having 3-6 months of living expenses saved.

*

Personal financial health, just like physical health, is about breaking habits that don't serve you well and creating and continuing healthy money habits. As a young professional, now is a great time to create good habits that will last throughout your career. Starting these habits young will increase your ability to retire comfortably and live the life you want. This article gives some great suggestions on habits to start today. The two that caught my eye were "Hang out with high-achievers" and "Get comfortable with discomfort." **https://www.cnbc.com/2018/07/05/habits-to-start-if-you-want-to-get-rich.html?__source=yahoo%7Cfinance%7Cheadline%7Cstory%7C&par=yahoo&yptr=yahoo**

Checks are not as common as a form of payment as they once were, but they can be useful in certain situations. One of our clients recently had to send a check in the mail. When the recipient told the client that they hadn't yet received the check, the client decided to cancel the check and send a new one. Little did she know, her bank charged her $30 to put a stop on the check.

Most banks will charge you a fee to cancel payment on a check. If you're willing to pay the fee, you need information including the check number, the exact amount the check was written for, your bank account number, and who the check was written to. If the check is a cashier's check, it cannot be canceled. It's important to be aware of the fees that your bank will charge you for certain services, as there are many fees for many things that you may not be aware of until it's too late.

*

Rule of 72

Ever wonder how long it will take for your money to double? Calculating the doubling period will help you estimate about how long it takes to save for a goal, for example, for a house down payment. The rule of 72 works like this:

Divide 72 by the rate of return you're getting on a savings or investment account. That tells you how many years it will take for the amount you have saved or invested to double.

For example, if you have $7,500 and it earns a 5% return, it will take 14.40 years to double or 10.2875 years to double at 7%.

*

Additional Resources

Here's a quick article on the time value of money, and why that $50 dinner tonight might be costing you more than you think. **https://www.thebalance.com/you-re-spending-your-millions-1-at-a-time-356374**

GOAL SETTING

Interesting Factoid

According to Facebook, Millennials are redefining financial success. Some 46% believe that financial success means being debt free. Owning a home was considered a top priority by 21% of Millennials, while only 13% cite being able to retire as their main financial priority. What do you define as financial success?

*

New year, new you, right? A great New Year's Resolution would be to set *a life goal* for yourself this year. Something like pursuing a certification that will help you advance in your career, or visiting family and friends on the other side of the country that you haven't seen in years. Once you have your life goal set, putting money aside for it will be much easier. Without goals, our money has no purpose. Remember: No Lazy Assets! Therefore, give your money some purpose and set out to achieve a life goal this year. New Year here we come!

*

Whether they are goals for health, finance, or fun, having SMART goals will help set you up for success. Here is what SMART goals are:

Specific – Choose goals that are specific. For example, "I want to put $100 per month into my savings account" is much more specific than "I want to save more."

Measurable – A goal that is measurable allows you to know exactly when it has been achieved. "I am going to go to the gym 3 days a week" can be measured, whereas "I want to get into shape" is too vague.

Achievable – It's great to have high hopes, but don't set yourself up for failure by having unrealistic expectations. Taking small steps by having reasonable, achievable goals will help you take small steps in the right direction. For example, saying "I want to be a millionaire by the end of this year" is probably too big of a leap for such a short time. Instead, "I want to have $25,000 in my bank account by the end of the year" might be more achievable to start.

Relevant – Choosing a goal that is meaningful to you will keep you motivated and it will feel much more fulfilling once achieved. If your goal is to buy your own home one day, your short-term goal might be to save for a down payment by XX date. If you may already own a house, your goals may be to pay off your car loan by December 31, XXXX or fully fund your 401(k) plan for the year.

Timed – Giving yourself a set time period will prevent you from procrastinating, making the achievement of your goal more likely. For example, saying "I want to pay off my student loan by July 31" gives your goal some structure, and also then helps you to figure out what you need to do each month in order to make that happen.

Once you've determined your goals, **take action on at least two of them within 48 hours**. Research shows that taking action creates momentum and that makes attaining the goal more likely. Before you know it, your time will be up, and you will have achieved your goal.

Here are some examples of SMART goals related to personal finance:

- Eliminate all my student debt by December 31, 2020;
- Save enough for a down payment on a house by June 1, 2025;
- Start a college savings program for both of our kids by March 31 and save $150/month for each.

If you're married or in a committed relationship, it's important to talk to your partner about your financial goals as a couple. You may find that you and your partner have very different goals in mind. Take some time to discuss your short-term and long-term goals with each other. You can't move forward with your goals until you are both on the same page. If this is something you haven't discussed before, you might be surprised to hear the other person's perspective.

Your partner may have ideas that you've never considered. You might also disagree on things. This may mean making some compromises. In the end, if you've set goals that are specific, measurable, attainable, realistic, and time-specific and are in agreement with your partner about these goals, then you're heading in the right direction.

*

About mid-year is a good time to ask yourself how your New Year's resolutions are going. So if it's July, are you still working towards completing the goals you set in January? Have you completely forgotten about them? Do you keep putting things off? If you've gotten away from the goals, there is still time. Review and re-commit. Now!

*

Although money usually helps us achieve our goals, not all goals are financial. It's important to include some goals in your life that don't require money. Maybe you've wanted to complete that half marathon, or go visit that beautiful landmark near your home that all the tourists visit, that the locals seem to forget about. Setting and completing these small life goals will help you feel satisfied, regardless of your financial situation.

*

According to a Wells Fargo survey, 58% of Millennials say they have enough money to pay for future needs. Additionally, the most intimidating money challenges for those surveyed were saving for the future, followed by knowing how to invest. Saving for the future and knowing how to invest go hand-in-hand. These dilemmas can be simplified so they are more approachable and not so intimidating. First, set SMART goals for yourself so that you know exactly the goals for which you're saving. This could be an emergency fund, savings for the down payment on a house, or saving for your Financial Freedom Day (retirement). Next, begin saving consistently and regularly for your goals every month or even every paycheck.

If you can set aside your savings right off the top before you have a chance to spend the money, rather than save whatever is leftover at the end of each month, you'll be adding to your future savings and won't notice the money was ever gone.

Investing does not have to be intimidating, but sometimes there isn't always a one size fits all answer for investing either. If your goal is an emergency fund, keep this money in a savings account, ideally one that pays at least 1% interest. If your goal is financial freedom and your company offers a 401(k) plan, contribute to that as much as possible, ideally 15% or more of your gross pay. To invest this money, choose a target date fund that corresponds to the year you'll turn 50 or so and the fund will invest it for you accordingly.

*

In another study, a report by Goldman Sachs listed eight things that Millennials want and don't want. Some of this data was not surprising. For example, Millennials are reluctant to make big purchases like buying a home or purchasing a car. Instead, they're ok with renting or living with their parents and using ride-share services. Another piece of not-so-surprising information was that Millennials value eating healthy and exercising. Millennials also care more about price than quality.

We started wondering why this information about Millennials was so important and realized that this is what makes our generation different than others. It hadn't occurred to us that previous generations highly valued things like homeownership, purchasing a car, or owning a designer luxury bag. Previous generations hadn't been as health-conscious as our generation. Once we put it in perspective, we realized that this is what makes our generation unique. This data story was eye-opening to us not so much for the data it revealed, but more so for how this information compares to other generations. What do you think? Are you surprised by the things Millennials want?

Chelsea Says:

If you're anything like me, you've got lots of goals and are super motivated, but lack the money to put towards funding those ambitions. Consider a side hustle. Drive for Uber, referee youth sports on the weekends, or if you're creative start an Etsy shop where you can sell your creations that probably originated as just a hobby. If you're a good speaker, consider becoming a wedding officiant, write a book, or even share your knowledge by teaching a few courses at the local college.

Any little extra money you make should first go towards paying off any debt, like student loans and credit cards. Then once your debts are paid off, put that extra money towards saving for your short, medium, and long-term goals. Harness that entrepreneurial spirit of yours and find a side hustle. You probably won't make a career out of it, but you'll definitely make some extra money.

There are more benefits to finding a side hustle than just extra money. Take a quick look at this link to discover a few more reasons why a side hustle might be a great choice for you.
http://www.bankrate.com/finance/personal-finance/5-rewarding-reasons-take-second-job.aspx

Chelsea Asks:

Kyle and I were discussing an article in the **Puget Sound Business Journal** that shows that to be considered wealthy in the Seattle area, people felt they needed to have a net worth of $4.26M. Whereas, the national standard is a net worth of $2.44M. Of course, this doesn't include other measurements of wealth such as good health, close relationships, happiness, etc., but what this shows is that wealth is relative.

Kyle asked me what my wealth number was, and I honestly had never thought about it before. So, now I ask you, what's your wealth number? Would your number ever change depending on the circumstances? Have you ever thought about it before?

Additional Resources

Here are some ways to help you set goals in a way that makes you more likely to achieve them. **https://www.mindtools.com/pages/article/newHTE_90.htm**

This article explains the science behind why we procrastinate and gives some really useful tips on how to avoid putting things off. Don't read this article later, read it now. **http://jamesclear.com/akrasia**

CAREERS

Obviously, your money is very important from several aspects. For one, it's what allows you to achieve your goals and create the life you want. But even more important is where your money comes from... your career! We're not career counselors; however, let us share our experience and please remember this:

The number one money mistake most early career professionals make is that they trade their time for money doing something they don't like to do.

Discover your strengths, discover what you enjoy doing and use those to create a career path for yourself. More than likely, you'll be more successful if you're doing something you love.

*

As an early career professional, you were probably very happy when you landed your first real job after college. But more than likely you won't stay at that job forever. How do you go about changing jobs when the time comes? First, you need to analyze **why** you're thinking about changing jobs. Did you have a bad day at work? Do you get along with your colleagues? Are you being challenged enough? Understanding your motivations will help you to choose a new job that fulfills your needs that aren't currently being met.

Next, research the jobs or new industries in which you're interested. Are your skills transferrable? Will you have to take a pay cut? Is the work/life balance what you're looking for? Once you've narrowed things down, discuss your aspirations with someone you trust, like a friend or family member. They can give you some honest feedback from an outside perspective that you may not have seen from within. Finally, make a decision. Either decide to change jobs or decide to stay at your current job. Don't let yourself stay in limbo. Make your decision and get back to being productive.

Chelsea Says:

I was very selective when searching for jobs before I found this one. I knew that I had a specific vision of what I wanted to be doing and did my best to weed out jobs that did not match that vision. It can be a long, hard process to find the right job with the right company in the right industry. In the end, changing jobs or careers is a major life challenge and the extra time and effort put into finding a good fit will be worth it when you're enjoying what you do every day

Additional Resources

Here's an article with five questions to consider before changing jobs. It points out how networking and image can affect the job changing process. Take a look. **http://money.usnews.com/money/blogs/outside-voices-careers/articles/2016-03-28/5-questions-to-ask-yourself-before-making-a-job-change**

This is a summary of the article "IDENTIFY YOUR SILVER LININGS: WANT TO CHANGE JOBS" (a 4-step decision making process for young professionals thinking about changing jobs) by Mark Howley **https://www.linkedin.com/pulse/identify-your-silver-linings-want-change-jobs-4-step-decision-howley**

SPENDING PLANS

Many people think they need a *budget* to get a handle on their money, but we don't like the term "budget." It feels too restrictive. Like a diet. The idea of a budget feels like a long list of things you can't do. Instead, we like a *spending plan*. A spending plan is open and abundant — it's your plan so you can choose how to allocate your income. The key to a successful spending plan is to spend on the things you love and ignore the rest. If you love to eat out, then do so; love shoes, buy them. But keep in mind that you will need to choose NOT to spend on something else that you don't love as much.

*

You've probably seen the headlines recently that a six-figure salary in San Francisco is considered low-income. As crazy as it sounds, this shows that it's not about how much you make but how much you spend. Cost of living is a major factor affecting personal financial success. That's why it's important when considering a new job to not just think about what your salary might be, but how the cost of living for that job will affect your finances.

A recent Money magazine article took the median income from each state and adjusted it based on purchasing power, to give the 'real' median income for the state. For example, the median income in Washington is $64,129. The price parity score for Washington was 104.8, meaning that prices are 4.8% higher than the national average. Therefore, Washington's median income has a real value of $61,192. The state with the highest price parity score, Hawaii, had a median income of $73,486, but when adjusted for purchasing power the real median income was just $61,857. The state with the lowest price parity score, Mississippi, had a median income of $40,593. Yet when adjusted for purchasing power the real median income rose to $47,092. These numbers show that it's not just salary that matters. If you can do your same job and get paid the same amount yet live in a location with a lower cost of living, you can increase how far your salary will go.

Check out the link below to see how the purchasing power in your state might affect your income.
http://time.com/money/5177566/average-income-every-state-real-value/

*

Bill Jenkins, a financial writer for MSN Money, suggests the 60% Solution as a spending plan. He proposes that you split your money into five categories:

- 60% Basic expenses (food, bills, taxes, etc.)
- 10% Retirement savings
- 10% Long term savings (house down payment, other large savings goals)
- 10% Short term savings for irregular expenses
- 10% Fun money

*

Here's another spending plan that Ramit Sethi suggests in his book "*I Will Teach You to be Rich*" (a terrific book):

50%--60%	Fixed costs (rent, utilities, debt, etc.)
10%--20%	Investments like 401(k) plan
5%-10%	Savings for vacations, gifts, house down payment, unexpected expenses
20%--30%	Guilt-free spending for dining out, movies, clothes, shoes

*

Want a really simple spending plan. Try this:

$$\text{Income} - \text{Savings} = \text{Spending Amount}$$

Shoot for at least 15% of your pre-tax earnings to save for your financial freedom day (used to be called "retirement"). You have to pay off your credit cards every month too. No cheating by buying something on credit and paying it off next month.

*

If you want to refine your spending plan, then you need to know where your money is going every month. If you use mobile banking, your bank's app may have a tracker function, which helps you see where your money is being used. My mobile bank allows me to see how much I spend on food & dining, auto & travel, shopping, etc. Or you can try one of the online expense tracking apps like Mint (**www.mint.com**) or YNAB (**www.youneedabudget.com**).

*

Most people track their monthly spending, and save whatever they have that's left over. But if you don't have much money left over, changing habits can be hard. A different strategy that encourages saving is to save money right off the top. Once you've put that money into savings, any leftover money can go towards your spending plan. You'll be less likely to feel restricted, and you'll feel good about putting your savings first. For long-term goals like your Financial Freedom Day, a good benchmark to shoot for is saving 15% of your **gross income**. (gross income is the amount you're paid before taxes and insurance are taken out of your paycheck). And for intermediate goals, like a home down payment or saving for a new car, saving 10% of your gross income is a good target.

*

At holidays, many people give gifts to family, friends, and even neighbors. Well before the holiday season starts is the time to start thinking about buying gifts for everyone. If you wait until the last minute, the purchases can really add up if you're not careful. Planning ahead will allow you to make well-thought out buying decisions and can help prevent you from overspending. This article does a great job of explaining tips on how to spend wisely and avoid the stress that can come with holiday gift buying. Some important steps included in this article are to:

1. Begin with a list of holiday expenses
2. Decide on your spending limit
3. Make a shopping list
4. Track your spending

Planning ahead is a great strategy to help you stay on track. If you're able to follow the spending plan you create for yourself, you'll feel much more relieved and accomplished after all the shopping has been done. **https://www.thebalance.com/how-to-stick-to-your-holiday-budget-2385688**

Chelsea Says:

Having a spending plan is a great way to ensure that you stay within your means. But if you're like me, lots of things pop up that are unexpected, can't be planned for, or are even seasonal. Things like kids' birthday parties, last minute invites to baseball games or roller skating, and attending summer camps. These expenses can really add up if you're not careful. I personally have learned that I don't need to spend a ton of money on birthday presents, as most kids are just as happy with a gift that costs $10 as they are with one that costs $30. I have also learned that summer camps are great to break up the monotony of summer, but aren't necessary for every single week.

> ## *Chelsea Says*:
>
> While I keep gift costs to a minimum in our spending plan, I also think it's a good idea to have a small buffer in your spending plan for these things, just in case. But it's also important to be able to say "no", especially to your kids. Just because they want to go to the baseball game or movies with friends doesn't mean they have to go.

Additional Resources

Do you have trouble sticking to a "budget"? At the **Financial Foundations Program** we recommend *spending plans*, not budgets. Our preferred approach is the 50/30/20 method, but this article also gives a good, simplified alternative to that as well. The key is to pick an approach that best fits you and STICK WITH IT. **https://www.thebalance.com/dont-like-tracking-expenses-try-the-80-20-budget-453602**

The first real step to taking care of your money is to track where your money is going, and how it's being spent. This sometimes sounds like a pain to do, but there are apps and websites available to help you make this very simple. Tracking your spending can be eye opening, and you might learn a few things about your spending habits that you didn't even realize you were doing.

Take a look. **http://www.lifehack.org/482228/5-surprising-benefits-of-tracking-your-spending**

TAKING CARE OF YOUR DEBT

If you're married, you and your spouse each have your own, separate credit scores. If you plan to buy a house or a car together, the lender will take both scores into consideration. Part of planning ahead when making big purchases like this is to look into each of your credit scores ahead of time and put in the work to raise those scores before you make a large purchase.

*

According to one survey, most early career professionals feel knowledgeable about credit, yet a third don't know their credit scores. The reality is that you are NOT knowledgeable about credit without knowing your credit score.

This website has a great infographic that shows what young professionals think about credit vs. the reality of their credit. **http://www.experian.com/blogs/ask-experian/millennials-and-credit-survey-results/**

*

Here's a link to five important things to know about your credit score. Check it out. Is there anything on this list that surprises you?

http://www.bankrate.com/finance/credit/millennials-and-credit-5-things-to-know-1.aspx

*

Many people get confused and think that their credit *score* and credit *report* are the same thing. They aren't. Each has a different role to play in your financial life.

A **credit score** is calculated using the information from your credit report. There are a few companies that calculate credit scores, such as FICO and VantageScore. Both use the 300-850 scale, with 850 being better credit. There are five weighted categories that are used to compute your score. Payment history makes up 35% of the score, amounts owed 30%, length of credit history 15%, credit maximum 10%, and new credit 10%.

You can access your credit score for free by visiting **www.creditkarma.com.** One way to improve your credit score is to make sure that you are keeping your utilization rate low. For example, if you have three credit cards and their limits add up to $10,000, then you want to keep your utilization below $3,000 for the three cards combined. Because this category is weighted heavily, improving your utilization can have a big impact on your score. Or if you have missed a payment or two in the past, put your accounts on an automatic payment system so that you don't ever miss a payment again.

The **Financial Foundations Program** team has prepared a special report on "How to Raise Your Credit Score" that offers more tips and suggestions on ways to improve this important number in your financial life. You can get a free copy of the report by contacting either Kyle (**kyle@finpath.com**) or Chelsea (**Chelsea@finpath.com**).

---

*

Three Quick Tips to Prioritize Your Debt

We often talk about debt and how to avoid it. But if you have debt and want to do something about it, below are three tips on how to start digging yourself out of the debt hole.

1. Address credit card debt and debt on depreciating assets, like cars, first. Most student loans have lower interest rates, and unlike consumer loans (credit cards, car loans), up to $2,500 of interest payments on student loans are tax deductible.

2. There are two options for paying off debt: the Avalanche Method and the Snowball Approach. With the *Avalanche Method* of paying off credit cards, you arrange your debts by **interest rates**, highest to lowest. Allocate the largest payment towards the debt with the highest rate, while making the minimum payment on the remaining cards. This will save you the most amount of money in the long run, as you will pay off your card with the highest interest rate first, and then continue to the card with the next highest rate until they've all been paid off.

   The *Snowball Method* is when you arrange your debts by **account balance**, lowest to highest. Allocate the largest payment towards the debt with the smallest balance, while making the minimum payment on the remaining cards. This way you see card balances go to zero more quickly and has the benefit of seeing great progress rapidly. Choose whichever method is the most consistent with your values.

3. Do not cancel your credit cards once they're paid off. Unless there's an annual fee, you'll want to keep these credit card accounts open because closing them can negatively affect your credit

score. If you're afraid you might use the card if the account remains open, cut the card up and pretend like the account doesn't exist. But be 100% sure it's paid off before doing so!

Paying off debt can take some time, so be patient. Once it's complete you'll feel relieved to not have that pesky debt monkey on your back. And going forward, it's important to address the spending behaviors that may have gotten you into debt in the first place. Changing those behaviors will allow you to continue on your debt-free financial path.

*

In 2017 Equifax, one of the three credit reporting agencies, had a security breach and millions of consumers' personal information was compromised. When these security breaches occur, regardless of what company is involved, it's important to know how to protect yourself and your identity.

Checking your credit report frequently is a great way to keep an eye on whether or not your identity has been stolen. If you see accounts open that you know you did not open or have accounts in collection that you know are not yours, these are some warning signs that you might be a victim of identity theft. Also, if you see transactions in your bank accounts that are not yours, that is a red flag that someone else has access to your information.

You can check your credit by visiting **www.annualcreditreport.com**, where you can receive one free credit report from each of the three credit agencies each year. Rather than receiving your credit reports from each of the credit agencies all at one time, a great strategy to monitor your credit is to visit this website once every four months and receive your credit report from one of the credit agencies. That way you can spread out your free reports throughout the year.

It is important that you protect your identity for many reasons. First, if someone opens accounts in your name and then does not pay these accounts back, you are responsible. The bill collectors will call you and calls from them are not pleasant. Second, this will negatively affect your credit score. When you have accounts in collections and don't pay them off, your score will go down and make it difficult for you to qualify for loans or credit in the future. Once your score goes down, it can be difficult and take a lot of hard work to get your score back up.

There are also other ways your identity can be stolen, including tax identity theft and medical identity theft.

You can see why it's important to be diligent in protecting your personal information, including social security numbers, bank account numbers, and even credit card offers through the mail. Do your best to prevent identity theft by carefully reading bank and credit card statements, then shredding statements, and monitoring your credit report.

*

For identity theft, prevention does not guarantee safety. You may be a victim due to a major data breach or hack. So what do you do then? We've gotten this question a great deal over the last few months ever since the Equifax data breach, but also when other companies have been hacked. You can put either a freeze on your credit, lock your credit, or use fraud alert services.

There are pros and cons to freezing your credit. On the plus side, freezing your credit gives you peace of mind because NO ONE can apply for credit using your personal information, not even you. On the con side of the ledger, you have to temporarily remove the freeze if you need to have a credit check done, for example, if you apply for a new credit card or lease a car. Some would say what's a few dollars to protect their credit?

Note: in September 2018, it became possible to freeze your credit and thaw it without fees. See the special section later on in this book on how to freeze credit.

Besides freezing your credit, there are other options to protect your credit including fraud alert services or a credit lock. A fraud alert service instructs creditors to verify your identity before issuing credit. Fraud alert services are free, but last for only 90 days. A credit lock is like a freeze, but has some differences. While a credit freeze is guaranteed by law, a credit lock is just an agreement between you and the credit agency. A credit lock also takes less time to implement and remove and is free from two of the three credit bureaus. There is not one single, correct answer to the problem of identity theft. It depends on your personal situation.

Chelsea Says:

The first time I ever saw my credit report was when my husband and I went to buy our first house. The mortgage broker asked me to review the credit report to make sure everything was correct. I was surprised when I saw the Nordstrom credit card I had opened my freshman year of college because I had forgotten I even had the card. There were no errors on my report and we proceeded in purchasing the house. But seeing my credit history all laid out like that was still eye-opening.

STUDENT LOAN DEBT

Student loan debt feels like a heavy ball and chain following you wherever you go, holding you back figuratively and literally. With the average college graduate having $37,000 in student loans upon graduation, that amount of debt early on in life can prevent you from accomplishing your goals. It will be more difficult for you to secure other types of loans, whether that is a business loan to create a new start-up, or a home loan if you're more inclined to settle down and start a family. Having this debt right out of the gate will hold you back.

As much as you might like to stick your head in the sand about your student loan debt, it's important to get to know your loans. How many loans do you have? Are they Federal student loans or private? For how long is each loan? At what interest rate is each loan? Knowing the details of your loans is the first step to creating a strategy to pay them off quickly and efficiently.

If you have Federal student loans, log into the **National Student Loan Data System**. If you have private student loans, check your credit report. You can get a free copy of your credit report at **AnnualCreditReport.com.**

*

To make it easier to repay your student loans, you can consider *consolidation* and/or *refinancing*. Some people confuse the terms. They are not the same thing. Federal student loans and private loans have different options.

You can **_consolidate_** Federal student loans. This is the process of combining multiple loans into one new loan. The US. Department of Education offers a Direct Consolidation Loan (DSL), which combines your federal loans into one new loan. The new interest rate is a weighted average of the interest rates of your old loans.

Generally, it's easy to qualify for a DSL and it has the advantage of simplicity because you're making one loan payment a month instead of multiple loans. You can enroll in income-driven repayment plans and you'll qualify for various forgiveness programs.

However, you might not save any money because the interest rates of your current loans are averaged to create the new loan rate. If you're interested in a DSL, go to **www.studentloans.gov** and look for the direct loan consolidation application.

You have the option to _**refinance**_ private student loans. When you refinance, a lender gives you a new loan with a new interest rate or term to replace the previous loans. Refinancing may save you money because you reduce your interest rate and it may allow you to shorten or lengthen the time period during which you're paying loans. As a result, you may lower your monthly payments and/or reduce the amount in interest you pay on your loans. However, in order to refinance private loans, you must meet eligibility requirements and that may mean you won't qualify. Lenders will look at your credit score (there's that term again!), income, savings and degree or certificate. Finding a bank to refinance private student loans is not easy and confusing. Make sure you do a good Internet search for articles on best banks to use and compare rates and terms.

We never suggest that someone refinance a Federal student loan because that gives up significant options like loan forgiveness for public service.

*

Consider using a **Student Loan Forgiveness Programs.** As many as 50% of borrowers qualify for some type of student loan debt forgiveness. To qualify, you must perform volunteer work, perform military service, practice medicine in specific communities, or meet other criteria. See if your state has a student loan forgiveness program and there are many other programs out there. In mid-2018, the website **Student Loan Hero** published what they call the "complete list of student loan forgiveness programs and options." Check it out at **https://studentloanhero.com/featured/the-complete-list-of-student-loan-forgiveness-programs/**.

*

Five simple tips to pay off your student loan debt faster:

1. Create a student debt repayment plan with specific goals and time frames.
2. Consider loan forgiveness programs.
3. Refinance private loans if it makes sense by obtaining a lower interest rate or better terms.
4. Pay the loan with the lowest balance off first. Make minimum payments on the rest. Then when the first loan is paid off, use the amount you were paying on that loan and add it to the

next loan. Continue this process until all of your loans are paid off. It's tempting to pay off the loan with the highest interest rate first, but psychologically, you'll benefit more by seeing progress on the loan balance going down rapidly on the smallest loan.

5. Consider a side hustles to earn extra money until your student loan debt is eliminated.

And one more bonus tip: when all your student loan debts are paid off, have a party!

*

The struggle to pay off student loan debt while still contributing to your 401(k) is real. And many employers recognize that their younger employees are having difficulties with this. That's why a recent IRS private letting ruling is making headlines. The IRS is now allowing employers to make matching contributions to an employee's 401(k) plan account if the employee makes student loan repayments of at least 2% of eligible compensation for the pay period. So to make it simple, if you make a student loan payment, your company can match your student loan payment (up to 5% of eligible compensation) with contributions to your 401(k) plan account.

Keep an eye out within your company to see when this might be an available employee benefit for you. **https://www.marketwatch.com/story/irs-ruling-allows-401k-student-loan-benefits-2018-08-27**

*

Avoid "get out of student loan" scams that could put you further into debt. Debt relief companies are almost always a bad idea. They usually make a sales pitch that sounds too good to be true and it is! Most debt relief companies are out to make money off of you and working with one may actually make your student loan debt worse, not better. Knowing that most debt relief companies are a bad idea, if you still feel the need to consider one, please take the following actions:

1. Check out the company with the Better Business Bureau. Do your homework on the company!

2. Make sure you understand any documents you're asked to sign and consider hiring an attorney to review any documents as well.

3. Don't make any payments to the company until you understand if the money you pay the company goes to pay off your student loan debts first. Some programs use the majority of your early payments to cover their fees first

with the minimum going to reduce student
loan balances.

4. If the company asks for a large up-front
    payment; that should be a red flag. Avoid this
    kind of arrangement.

Always consider your own debt relief program first
before you turn to a debt relief company. They will
promise you anything and make bold half-truth and
misleading statements to get you to trust them and to
get your money and it's almost always a bad idea. Buyer
beware!

Additional Resources

There are many rules and regulations with student loans,
and just like any other loan it's important to be as well-
informed as possible before signing on the dotted line.
Processes such as loan forbearance, consolidation, and
loan forgiveness often have many strings attached, so
it's important to be aware of the fees and rules that go
along.

This article gives some unfortunate examples of people who didn't know the rules and ended up with 3-4 times more debt than which they initially started.
https://www.cnbc.com/2018/05/05/for-some-student-loan-debt-is-doubling-tripling-and-even-quadrupling.html

EMERGENCY SAVINGS

A great way to jump start or give a boost to your emergency savings is to use your tax refund or any bonuses you may receive from work, to add to your emergency savings account, especially if it's money you didn't anticipate having. Your emergency savings should be in an account that maintains its value and won't charge you anything to withdraw from.

Visit **Bankrate.com** to check out the high-yield savings accounts offered by the Internet banks listed on the website.

Here's a great article about how to start an emergency fund, where to keep your emergency fund, and a few reasons why an emergency fund is so important. Check it out **https://blog.mint.com/saving/6-steps-to-starting-an-emergency-fund-0413/**

*

Six out of ten Americans don't have enough money to cover an unplanned $500 expense, according to a recent CNN Money article. This is a chilling statistic. Do you have a dog? A car? A house? Many things can happen unexpectedly: a veterinarian bill, a flat tire, a broken furnace. Having an Emergency Savings fund will ensure that you can cover these costs.

The best way to begin is to start small. First, set your goal at $500. Ideally, you would put money into your savings account immediately after being paid. Having money automatically transferred into your savings account once a month is a great way to do this. Then once you've reached your goal of $500, increase your goal to $1,000. Eventually, you'll want to have 3-6 months' worth of living expenses saved in your Emergency Savings fund. If you lose your job, you have money to live off of until you find another job.

Having an Emergency Savings fund is important because it prevents these unexpected expenses from growing. Without savings, you may be forced to charge the expense to a credit card, and it may be hard to come out from under that.

*

Saving money doesn't have to be hard. With the advancement of technology, automated savings does all the hard work for you.

Whether it is saving for retirement in your 401(k) account, emergency savings, saving for your children's education, or saving for a vacation, automating your savings ensures that the proper amount is saved each and every month. If you wait to save your money until the end of the month, you're more likely to dip into that money if it's sitting in your checking account. Having the money transferred automatically prevents you from overspending. Saving to your 401(k) or 403(b) plan account is automatically deducted from your paycheck. If your company offers you the opportunity to purchase company stock at a discount, these purchases can be automatically deducted from your paycheck as well. If you're working on an emergency savings, set up an automatic transfer from your checking account each month. You'll slowly start to see your savings accounts increase and you won't notice that money was ever taken from your checking account.

*

When Is It Okay to Tap Your Emergency Fund?

So you have an emergency fund started. Good for you. The next question to answer is "When is it okay to use your emergency fund?" In addition to using it for when something BIG happens – like to cover your living expenses if you lose your job -- your emergency fund can also be used when you have a smaller unexpected life event. For example, if your car breaks down or your furnace stops working qualify as emergencies. Emergency funds should only be used if absolutely necessary. This means that even though you might **want** to take a vacation, that's not what we mean by an **emergency.**

If you use some of your emergency fund, be sure to commit to bringing your emergency fund back up to the proper level in the following months. The money is there for you to use when a sudden and usually negative event happens so it's okay if you need to use it. Just be sure that you replenish the fund as quickly as possible afterwards.

BUYING A CAR

Buying a car can seem complicated and intimidating and can have significant consequences if not properly planned for. That's why doing research and planning ahead is the best way to ensure you don't make any big mistakes or act on impulsive decisions that many people do when buying a car. Some people pay all cash for their car, others take out a loan and still others sign a lease. If you need to borrow money to help purchase a car, credit unions are a great place to start.

The first step is to become pre-qualified for a car loan. A rule of thumb is the 20/4/10 rule. That is, you should put at least 20% as a down payment on your car. Your loan term should not be longer than 4 years, and your monthly payment (principal, interest, and insurance) should not be more than 10% of your gross income. Using these guidelines, you can determine how much of a loan for which you qualify.

Or perhaps you've heard that leasing is a good idea. When leasing, you typically have lower monthly payments, meaning you can drive a more expensive car than if you were to purchase a car. But, the disadvantages to leasing include limits to the number of miles you can put on the car, the expectation that the car stays very clean and well maintained, and that any types of door dings or extra mileage will cause you to incur fees when you return the car. The biggest disadvantage of a lease is that at the end of the lease, you don't have a car. Leases are tricky, so be sure you understand the lease document completely before you go this route.

Once you know how much car you can afford and how you're going to pay for it, you can do your research to ensure you find the best car for your money. You'll probably want to check for the car's reliability, cost-to-own (which includes maintenance costs and gas costs), and then finally check with your insurance company to see how much insurance will cost for you on that specific car. Using these guidelines and planning ahead can help you stay focused and stick to your priorities, because as you can probably guess, car salesmen will try to influence your decisions and they are experts in the art of influence.

*

Remember: use the 20/4/10 Rule for Car Loans: 20% down payment, 4 year maximum loan term, and car costs (payment + insurance) should be no more than 10% of your gross income.

Chelsea Says:

Looking back on my experience buying my first car, I can say I'm quite proud. My husband and I had just gotten married, and it was our first major purchase together. He was deployed to Iraq and trusted me to make most of the decisions. We had some money saved up, which we used for a down payment. I got pre-qualified for a loan, so I knew the price range that I was looking for. Then it came down to just searching the Internet every day to see what cars were available. My dad told me, "You're doing them (the car dealers) a favor by purchasing from them. If they don't give you what you want, you can take your money and go buy from the dealership down the road." With that in mind, I was confident that I wasn't going to get the run-around from the salesmen. I was patient and didn't buy the first car I test drove. We ended up buying a great car, which we paid off after 3 years and still have today.

Additional Resources:

Here's a link to some great tips when buying a car.
Everyone can benefit from checking out these
suggestions because buying a car is a major purchase
that can have long-term consequences if not planned for
properly. My personal favorite is tip #6: buy based on
purchase price, not monthly payments.
http://www.moneycrashers.com/how-to-buy-car-tips/

HAVING A BABY

Some life events have a major impact on our finances and others not so much. One of these life-changing events is having a baby. It is nearly impossible to be mentally or emotionally prepared for the many changes that occur when you become a parent. **But it is possible to be financially prepared**.

Here's a checklist of questions to consider that will help make sure all your bases are covered before baby comes along.

- If you're married, you will need to discuss with your partner whether or not one of you can stay at home with the baby while the other works, and live off of a single income.

- If you're single, you will need to think about how long you can afford to take maternity leave, and who will care for the baby once you go back to work.

- Married or single, if you return to work how much will your take-home pay be after daycare expenses are paid?

- How will having a baby affect your health insurance costs?

- Do you have a car big enough and safe enough to transport a baby in a car seat?

- If you die unexpectedly, who will take care of baby for you? Do you have a will that can ensure that your wishes for who will care for your child will be followed? If you don't have a will, then this will be decided by the state.

- If you die unexpectedly, will your child be taken care of financially? Do you have life insurance that will provide for your child the things that you would have, had you not died, like paying for their college or their wedding?

These are questions that you'll want to have answered before baby comes, as these issues will immediately affect your finances. Of course, there are future expenses that come along with having children, but we'll just take it one step at a time.

*

One of the biggest decision new parents have to make is if both parents will continue working and find good childcare, or if one parent should stop working in order to stay home with the baby. Financially, what this boils down to is choosing between lower income or higher expenses. If one parent decides to stay home, there is less money coming in, but also less money going out because there is no expense for childcare.

If both parents decide to work, then there will be higher expenses to go along with the dual income. In some states, infant care costs per year are the same as or greater than the cost for in-state 4-year public college tuition. For example, in Washington state infant care costs make up 18.5% of median family income. That's a large amount of your paycheck going towards one expense.

Regardless of which decision works for you and your family, it's important to create and stick with a spending plan. If one parent stays home, it's important to have a spending plan to allocate your limited income appropriately. If both parents work and childcare is required, a spending plan will ensure that the extra expense of childcare is a planned expense. Aside from childcare costs, having babies who grow into children brings on many other expenses that were not previously incurred. Creating and sticking to a spending plan will lay a good foundation no matter your situation.

Here's a great website that breaks down childcare costs by state. If you plan on having children, this website will help give you the information you need to decide whether working and paying childcare costs or staying home is the best choice for your personal situation. **http://www.epi.org/child-care-costs-in-the-united-states/**

Chelsea Says:

Having a baby is exciting, stressful, and scary -- all at the same time! When I had my first baby, I was fortunate enough to not really have to worry about finances. My husband was in the military, so we had great medical, and even got paid more for having a kid. My life wasn't worry-free though, as having a baby brings plenty of other things to worry about in addition to finances. As much as you try to prepare yourself for having your first child, unexpected events almost always happen. While it's important to have a positive outlook, it's also important to just be aware that things may not go as planned or that something will happen that is outside of your control.

For me, I had a very healthy pregnancy with my first son and delivery went fine. But after he was born, he was whisked away to the Neonatal Intensive Care Unit for breathing problems. He ended up having to stay there for 10 days, hooked up to an IV for antibiotics. Luckily for us, we had great medical insurance that covered his unexpected medical expenses. There was no way for us to plan for something like that. So when you find yourself expecting your first child, saving some extra money and making sure you have good health care insurance for unexpected expenses could really be a lifesaver.

Right now, we have a few clients who are expecting. I feel privileged to be able to listen to them voice their concerns about how having a baby will impact their finances and I have eased some of the stress and fear by creating plans for them that address the issues that having a baby brings. Having a financial plan may ease the financial worries, but becoming a parent will bring on many other stressors. Take some time to plan ahead financially before the baby arrives on the scene because you'll have plenty of other things to worry about once baby comes along.

https://www.nerdwallet.com/blog/health/15-financial-must-dos-to-prepare-for-a-new-baby/

Additional Resources:

When you're pregnant, a major financial consideration is childcare costs. Here's a great piece on the many aspects to consider when deciding whether the cost of childcare is worth it. If you don't have time to read the whole thing, skip to the topic that catches your eye. These include: Is the Cost of Childcare Worth It - The Bottom Line, Career Considerations, Social and Emotional Considerations, Lifestyle Considerations, Making It Work with Two Incomes, and Making It Work with One Income.

There's some great information about childcare cost rules of thumb, strategically planning your pregnancies to minimize childcare costs, and how staying home can affect your career. **http://www.doughroller.net/smart-spending/cost-of-childcare/**

KIDS AND MONEY

It's never too early to start teaching your children about money. For younger kids, playing store and teaching that different coins have different values is a fun game that sets the foundation for learning how money works. As children get older, you can allow your children to earn an allowance. The amount of the allowance and the work required to earn it are unique to your family. Once your child is earning an allowance, you can then teach him or her about the importance of saving, and how to spend their money thoughtfully. Some good rules of thumb are to save 50%, spend 40% and donate 10% to charity. This will be the foundation for teaching a child how to give purpose to each dollar they earn. At this point, you can take your child to the bank and open an account for them. If they're old enough you can teach them about interest, and how their money will grow if it's in an interest-bearing savings account.

*

We learned some of our money habits, both good and bad, by watching our parents. Therefore, if you have kids, watch what you do and say about money. They're watching and listening to you. A recent report points out that kids watch what their parents do much more than we think they do. Here's a fun exercise to try with your partner: ask him/her what their first money memories are from when they were growing up. You do the same. This little exercise might reveal something important about your money personality.

*

If you're planning on opening a savings account for your child, do some research to find the best savings account for kids because different banks offer different interest rates as well as other benefits. Here's a link with a list of some good children's savings accounts.
https://www.nerdwallet.com/blog/banking/kids-savings-accounts-nerdwallets-picks/

Also, look into a savings account at your local credit union. They can probably offer competitive interest rates, with the benefit of being able to take your child there in person so they can get the full banking experience.

*

5 Things to Remember about UGMAs

Ever hear of a UGMA? Maybe you even had one when you were a kid. A UGMA (Uniformed Gift to Minor Account) is an account created for the benefit of a child. Sometimes parents or grandparents will create a UGMA for a child in order to gift assets or money to the child. Here are five important things to know about UGMAs.

1. Assets placed in the account are for the benefit of the child and are effectively removed from the donor's estate.

2. Assets held in the account are managed by a custodian until the child reaches the age of consent, usually 18 or 21, but it is different for each state.

3. Once the child reaches the age of consent, the assets are the child's and they may use the assets however they choose.

4. Assets held in the account are not tax-free. The first $1,050 of unearned income, which is income from investments, is not taxed, the next $1,050 is taxed at the child's tax rate, and anything beyond $2,100 is taxed at the parents' marginal tax rate. (Note: these limits are as of 2018 and the limits are adjusted periodically by tax law; be sure to

check with a qualified tax expert before making any tax-related decisions.) Therefore, although the assets are removed from the parents' estate, they are still exposed to being taxed at a potentially high rate.

5. A disadvantage to a UGMA is that the assets in a UGMA will be included as the child's assets when applying for financial aid to attend college. Those assets will be included in the child's calculated expected contribution to pay for college, which may decrease the amount of aid for which the child qualifies.

*

At a recent team lunch, a coworker asked where people get their bad money habits from. This is a great question, as it touches on a somewhat new subject in the financial world, behavioral finance. Behavioral finance combines traditional psychology with economics to study why people make irrational financial decisions. There is a constant tug of war between nature vs. nurture, and it includes how we view and relate to money.

More often, we watch our parents and their relationship with money and form our habits, good and bad, through those experiences. This article does a great job of explaining how different experiences in our childhood can affect our financial habits as adults. As a parent, this article opened my eyes to potential situations that I may be in that could negatively influence my children. https://www.igrad.com/articles/childhood-money-habits-learned-from-parents

*

Kids are expensive. You may think you'll be saving money by scaling back on weekend getaways, or cutting back on eating out at fancy restaurants. Instead, you'll be spending that money on diapers, food, health care, and even extra housing costs if you need to find a new place with more bedrooms. According to CNN money, it costs $233,610 to raise a child born in 2015, about $13,000 per year. These costs vary depending on your location, with the urban Northeast being the most expensive, followed by the urban West, and rural areas throughout the country coming in least expensive.

Planning out everything takes time. You will need to first discuss all these topics and more with your partner, and come to an agreement about how to handle things.

From there you'll want to read up on your options. You'll probably do a lot of planning, reading and research, more planning, and then more reading. And don't forget to have fun! It's an exciting time, enjoy the process.

Chelsea Says:

My sons often receive gift cards and money as presents. If your children do too, take this opportunity to teach them about money. Take them shopping and help them find something they want to purchase that is within their "budget." Explain to them that if they spend all their money on candy, and eat all the candy that day, their enjoyment will be short-lived. Whereas if they buy a toy, that toy can bring enjoyment for much longer. Also, encourage them to save some of their money. *Note: Teaching them to save is a great way to also hold yourself accountable to save as well.*

Chelsea Says:

Both my kids have piggy banks in their room, and whenever they receive or earn money, they've become great at going straight to their room and shoving it in the piggy bank.

But I'll admit they do not have savings accounts...yet. My older son has asked me a few times recently, "Mom, when are you going to take me to the bank to get a savings account?" His persistence has spurred me to finally take them.

Additional Resources

Here's a great article on money lessons to teach your kids based on their age. It also gives suggestions on age-appropriate activities that help teach these lessons. Take a quick look and see what lessons you could be teaching your kids.
https://www.forbes.com/sites/laurashin/2013/10/15/the-5-most-important-money-lessons-to-teach-your-kids/#1f1026a68269

College can be costly. That's why our colleague, Amy Shappell CFP®, wrote a guide called **"10 Tips to Help Families Pay for College"** (you can get a copy by emailing **chelsea@finpath.com**). Over the past 10 years, the average rate of inflation for college tuition has been 5%. That rate is higher than both the general inflation rate and the personal income inflation rate. If you want to pay for college for your child completely, or even help pay for a portion, the best thing you can do is to plan ahead. As soon as your child is born, you can open a **529 college savings account** (see next tip below) for him or her and begin contributing.

But how much should you save? This all depends on what type of school your child attends. In the 2016-2017 school year, the average cost for tuition at a 2-year community college was $3,520, while the average annual cost for tuition at a 4-year private school was $33,480. The cost to attend an Ivy League school or Stanford is twice that. With such a wide range of costs, you'll need to decide on what type of school you'd be willing to pay for and save accordingly, or decide on a specific amount for which you'd be willing to pay and explain to your child that if the school they choose to attend is more expensive, then they will be responsible for the additional costs.

Based on a current tuition of $21,648 per year and 5% annual tuition inflation, a student attending a 4-year public university and enrolling in the year 2035 can expect to pay $208,390 for four years of college. Assuming that a 529 college savings plan earns 6% annual interest, the amount a parent would need to save over 18 years would be $538 per month.

If saving that much sounds daunting to you, request a copy of Amy's special report **"10 Tips to Help Families Pay for College"** to help ease the process. Amy managed to put two children through college and not leave them with massive debt, so her tips are straightforward, effective and practical. For a copy of Amy's report, you can contact **Chelsea@finpath.com**.

*

A **529 college plan** is a tax-advantaged account in which the funds are used for education expenses. We say it's "tax-advantaged" because money you put into the plan is not taxed when it comes out as long as it's used to pay for qualified expenses.

Note that when you take money out of a 529 plan, it is **tax free** (meaning you don't pay taxes on the earning on your contributions to the plan) and not tax-deferred like a 401(k) plan or IRA. Until recently, the money in 529 accounts could only be used for college, but with recent changes in the laws, up to $10,000 per year can now be used for K-12 education as well.

529 plans are state-sponsored. Each state has their own 529 plan with different investment options, different fees, and different restrictions. Regardless of where you live, you can open a 529 plan account through any state. It's also important to know that your child does not have to go to college in the state where the plan is sponsored. For example, you and your family could live in Virginia, open a state of Utah 529 plan account, and the beneficiary (typically your child) could use those funds to go to college in Montana.

There are two types of 529 plans: pre-paid tuition plans and education savings plan. The pre-paid tuition plan allows you to buy college credits at current tuition rates. This allows you to lock in on current tuition prices, avoiding the risk of rising tuition inflation. The education savings plan is like an investment account.

Contributions to these accounts are invested and grow tax-free so long as the money is used for qualified education expenses. Qualified education expenses include tuition, room & board, and books among others. Visit **www.savingforcollege.com** for more details on the benefits, rules and restrictions for 529 plans.

*

The published costs for college aren't always the price you'll pay; they're just the sticker price. Here are six ways to help you keep college costs low and avoid sticker shock.

1. Apply for Federal Student Aid (even if you don't think you'll qualify.) The form is available on Oct 1 of the year before the student begins school. Aid is given on a first come first served basis so apply as soon as possible. You can find the application at **www.fafsa.ed.gov**

2. While your student is in high school, encourage him/her to take classes that can count towards college credit, such as Advanced Placement (AP) classes or International Baccalaureate (IB) classes.

3. Attending a community college for two years then transferring to a four year university is a great way to save on tuition costs.

4. Encourage your student to graduate college on time. Taking longer to graduate increases overall costs significantly. Look for colleges that offer a "fast-track," where a student can graduate in three years. This can decrease costs by up to 25%.

5. If your student is going to college out of state, but still in your region of the country, check to see if the school is part of a Regional Interstate Compact for Higher Education. Colleges within a region may agree to give out-of-state students who are from within their region a discounted cost. For example, the Western Undergraduate Exchange includes more than 150 public institutions throughout 16 states in the western U.S. that allow out of state students to pay for college at 150% of the institution's resident tuition cost.

6. If your student is going to college near home, consider having them live at home and commute to school. You will save money on room and

board, but don't forget the costs of gas and car insurance.

Chelsea Says:

Recently, I was talking with my oldest son and the topic of college came up. He "informed" me that he would like to go to Stanford. I was surprised by this but also very proud that he had set his sights so high at such young age. The more time that I've had to think about it, the more I realize that I want to support him in his college pursuits, and in order to do this I may need to start saving more for his college education than I had realized. It may seem like your children are too young to know, but for those of you with kids, talk to them about these things. They may have thoughts and goals of which you were unaware.

However, the conversation with my son did shake me. "Stanford?" I decided it was time to finally open a 529 account for each of my kids. I did some research and found that the "**my529**" plan sponsored by the state of Utah was the best fit for me. It's also the one that we here at Juetten Personal Financial Planning recommend most often. The sign-up process was fairly easy; all I needed were my sons' social security numbers.

I chose age-based accounts, which means that when the child is younger there's more invested in stocks and as the child gets closer to age 18, the investments shift towards assets that maintain their value. The nice thing is that I didn't have to have any money to open the accounts. Now that the accounts are open, I can easily transfer money from my bank account to them. It was a very easy process, and I recommend anyone with children consider opening a 529 account.

Visit **www.savingforcollege.com** to learn about which 529 plan is best for you. Once you open a college savings account, you'll find yourself more likely to deposit money simply because you can.

BUYING A HOME

So you're thinking about buying a house. You've probably heard that you'll need money up front for a down payment and closing costs. But there are many other costs associated with buying a house. These include paying for a home inspection, taxes, and insurance.

A **down payment** is cash that goes towards the purchase of a house. The amount of your down payment can range from 5%-20% of the purchase price of your house, depending on what type of home loan you are using. Say you want to purchase a home for $250,000. A 10% down payment would require you to pay the seller $25,000 cash and then take a loan out for $225,000. Having a down payment gives the buyer the incentive to make the mortgage payments on time, because the down payment would be completely lost if the house goes into foreclosure. Also, the larger the down payment is, the smaller the monthly mortgage payments. This is because with a larger down payment, you are borrowing less from the bank.

Closing costs include many different types of fees, like an appraisal fee, inspection costs, escrow deposit for property taxes, upfront mortgage insurance, plus the realtors' commissions. This closing cost calculator from **www.smartasset.com** can help you determine how much you will pay up front to buy a home. Different states require different fees, so this calculator can help you figure out which costs are required for your location. Keep in mind that some of these costs are set, such as taxes and government fees, while other costs such as the home inspection and title services, can vary based on who you use for these services.

*

Keep in mind that many more expenses come with owning a home compared to renting. For example, if you own a dog and the house you buy does not have a fence, you will need money to have a fence installed. Depending on the size of your lot, this could cost thousands of dollars. Or, you may discover that your house does not have air conditioning and need to install an air conditioning unit. Plus, it is always a good idea to have money saved up for emergencies, such as if your furnace goes out or your refrigerator breaks. When you own a home all the responsibility falls on you, the homeowner.

Having this much cash on hand can take time to accumulate. It's important to put this money in a separate savings account, preferably a high-yield savings account. Most online banks offer savings accounts with interest rates near 2%. As you deposit money into this account, it will slowly grow with interest. If you're planning on buying a house, do the research early to find out how much money you will need up front. Then give yourself time to save. A great way to jump-start your savings is to designate any bonus money or tax return refunds towards your up-front costs savings.

*

If you're thinking about buying a home, here's a good rule of thumb to keep in mind: Housing costs shouldn't be greater than 33% of your net income.

*

Many early career professionals ask us if they should save to buy a home or just rent. Depending on where you live, home prices have dramatically increased. This means that saving enough for the down payment (10% is typical) looks daunting. For example, the median price of a home in Seattle is currently $722,000. So saving $72,000 for a down payment plus money for other upfront costs makes buying a house difficult. While on the other side of the state, the median price of a home in Spokane is about $205,000. The answer of whether to rent or buy is not clear cut and depends on your circumstances.

When deciding whether to buy or rent a house, there are many factors to consider. First are the upfront costs. When buying a home, your upfront costs will include a down payment, inspection and appraisal costs and closing costs. If you choose to rent, your upfront costs are usually first and last month's rent and a security deposit.

Next are the on-going costs. With home ownership, your on-going costs include your mortgage payment, property taxes, homeowners' insurance, private mortgage insurance, and utilities. For renting, your on-going costs include your rent, renters' insurance, and utilities (although sometimes some of these are included in the monthly rent you pay.)

The advantages of owning a home include tax deductions for the interest paid on your mortgage, as well as the possibility of your home increasing in value. The increase in value usually takes a few years, so it's important to see a home as a long-term investment. Homeowners are also able to personalize their home and their yard, through painting, remodeling, and landscaping choices that renters do not have.

The advantages of renting either an apartment or a home include being able to relocate much easier and not being responsible for any maintenance costs. If the furnace breaks, a renter only needs to tell the landlord, who will then pay someone to fix it, while a homeowner is responsible for paying for repairs.

There is no one-answer-fits-all for buying or renting a home. It all depends on your personal financial circumstances, your preferences, and future plans.

Chelsea Says:

Buying a home for the first time can be quite the experience. Even if you've done your research, unexpected things can happen. When we bought our first house, we were fortunate to not need a down payment because we were using a Veterans Administration (VA) loan.

I remember having to show proof of our income, which meant providing several months' worth of bank statements, pay stubs, and lots more paperwork.

Once we were approved for a loan, we had a family friend who was a realtor help us shop around for houses. Lucky for us, we found a house in our price range, in the neighborhood that we were hoping for. We came to an agreement on the purchase price with the sellers and started the escrow process. Each step of the way, our realtor kept us up to date on what was going on, as well as walked us through all the paperwork.

When it came time for the appraisal, we encountered some unexpected news. The house appraised for lower than the purchase price, so the seller was forced to lower the price to the appraisal price. This was great news for us! After a few more weeks of inspections and more paperwork, we closed on our house and moved in. That was exactly 8 years ago this month. Since then, we've had to install a new fence, AC unit, new refrigerator, and new furnace. The joys of being a homeowner!

Additional Resources

Are you considering buying a home? Here's a good article on renting versus buying, and different topics to consider before making the leap from renter to homeowner.
https://www.nerdwallet.com/blog/mortgages/buying-renting-real-cost-of-owning-a-home/

FINANCIAL FREEDOM DAY

"Retirement" sounds like something your grandfather did. Instead, let's call it "Financial Freedom Day". That's the day when you won't have to work; it's the day when you can choose what you do each day without regards to making a living. Financial Freedom Day is a chance to start something new, whether it is starting a business, continuing your education, or pursuing volunteer opportunities.

Did you know that in one survey 41% of people born between 1980 and 2000 said they plan to retire when they reach a financial milestone, as opposed to reaching a certain age? So if you think you're too young to think about *retirement*, instead think about your **Financial Freedom Day**. Imagine what would your life look like if you had enough money to live comfortably and had the freedom to do whatever you chose?

*

How to Start Saving for Your Financial Freedom Day

As an early career professional, Financial Freedom Day (aka retirement) is probably something you envision old people with grey hair worrying about. You think, "I'm young and I've got plenty of time to plan". And you're right, you have time. So use this powerful asset to your advantage; the earlier you start saving, the more time your account has to grow through compound earnings.

Most people have access to a retirement savings plan through their employer, either through a 401(k) or 403(b) plan. These plans take money from your earned income before you've paid taxes, and contribute them to an account where they can grow tax-free until you're ready to retire. Oftentimes, an employer will match your contribution up to a certain percentage of your income. (Who doesn't like free money?)

*

The other most common way people save for retirement is by opening an Individual Retirement Account (IRA). There are two types of IRAs: a **Traditional IRA** allows you to deduct the amount you contribute to this account from your taxable income, therefore reducing your current income taxes. Once you retire and start pulling money from the account, you pay taxes on these distributions. A **Roth IRA** addresses taxes in the opposite way. You can contribute money that has already been taxed into a Roth IRA and when you're ready to retire, you can pull that money out and not pay any taxes at that time.

The most you can contribute to a Traditional or Roth IRA in a year is $5,500 in 2018 (more for someone who is older than age 50). However, there are income limitations that may limit or prevent you from contributing to either a Traditional or Roth IRA. In 2018 for a Traditional IRA, if you are married and your modified adjusted gross income (MAGI) is less than $101,000, or if you are single and your MAGI is less than $63,000 you can receive a full tax deduction up to the amount of your contribution limit. For a Roth IRA, if you are married and your MAGI is less than $189,000, or you are single, and your MAGI is less than $120,000 you can contribute the full amount to a Roth IRA. If your MAGI is above these limits, the amount that can be deducted from taxes through a Traditional IRA, and the amount allowed to be contributed through a Roth IRA begins to phase out. (Note: the maximums and contribution limits change regularly so be sure to check with a qualified tax expert or source before contributing to an IRA.)

Traditional IRAs and Roth IRAs usually let you invest in mutual funds, stocks, bonds or ETFs. We recommend that you try to save at least 15% of your pre-tax salary into a tax deferred account every year. The advantage of these accounts is that growth within the accounts is not taxed, only distributions from them (except for Roth IRAs). There are many exceptions and rules for contributions and distributions so be sure to read up on those before you open any type of retirement account. The IRS has a good page for getting started. https://www.irs.gov/retirement-plans/individual-retirement-arrangements-iras

Here's a great article that explains the benefits of Roth IRAs for professionals just starting out: https://www.cnbc.com/2018/01/26/roth-iras-are-a-retirement-hack-millennials-will-love.html

*

Rule of thumb: Have one year's salary saved for retirement by age 35

*

According to one survey we saw, 66% of Millennials have nothing saved for retirement. With many Millennials having student loans, and the high cost of living in many places, there usually isn't much money leftover to be saved. A 2014 report from the National Institute on Retirement Security showed that Millennials are putting retirement savings off, instead saving whatever extra money they do have towards buying a home or paying off student loans.

If saving for retirement is a priority for you and your employer offers a 401(k) or 403(b) plan, be sure you are saving enough to maximize the employer matching amount. Ideally, you want to save at least 10%, preferably 15%, of your gross income towards retirement. If you aren't there yet, start by saving the minimum amount required to receive the company's total matching amount. Then each time you receive a pay raise, increase your retirement savings and you will reach that 10% amount in no time. Once there, continue increasing until you're saving 15% towards retirement.

If saving for retirement is not a current priority, that's fine. But it's important to understand that the longer you wait to save for retirement, the more money you will need to save in order to catch up. When you begin saving at a younger age, you have the power of compound interest on your side. Although your contributions may be small when you're young, they have more time to grow.

If you decide to wait to save for retirement, just be aware that your money has less time to grow, and therefore you may need to save more. You may also need to delay retirement and work longer in order to give your money as much time to grow as possible. It's up to you how you prioritize your financial goals. Just be sure you understand the long-term effects that waiting to save for retirement can have.

*

Have you ever thought about what it would take to retire at 40? Many people consider retiring at 62 years-old as young, so retiring at 40 seems like a crazy thought, right? Well, there's a trend among a small group of young professionals called FIRE. This stands for Financial Independence Retire Early. This group dials back their expenses so that they can save anywhere between 50%-75% of their income. By increasing their savings, they are able to save a large amount at a young age. Pair this with the power of compound interest received when investing at an early age and you have the right strategy for retiring at 40.

*

According to the Schwab Center for Financial Research, you would need to have 25 times your core living expenses saved in order to retire at any age. That is, if your yearly expenses are $60,000 you would need to have $1,500,000 saved. At that amount, you would be able to withdraw 4% of your retirement savings per year and have it last in perpetuity.

*

Let's say that you decide you want to retire at 40 and are successfully able to save enough. What's next? It's important to really think about what a typical day in your retirement will look like. For some, retirement doesn't mean not working at all, it just means being able to do work that you enjoy and not rely on a job for income (hence Financial Independence.) For others, retirement may mean traveling the world, in which case you'll have to strategically plan your retirement expenses to include travel costs.

You may even discover that retirement at 40 isn't all it's cracked up to be. And that's ok too. Research done by Maria Fitzpatrick and Timothy Moore, of Cornell University, has shown that men who retire young (begin receiving Social Security at 62 years old) have an increased mortality rate of 20%.

Further, research done by Oregon State University shows that for each year you work beyond age 65, you have an 11% lowered risk of death from all causes. Now, retiring early at 62 cannot be directly compared to retiring early at 40. But it's important to think about what you'll do in retirement, as that may directly impact your health, both mentally and physically.

Additional Resources:

Here's a great article that explains how saving for your Financial Freedom Day is different for everyone because everyone's situation is different. It has some great guidelines to help with determining your appropriate savings rate, and how it changes as you move forward. **https://www.moneyunder30.com/how-much-should-you-contribute-to-your-401k**

TAXES

Let's say you receive a tax refund from the IRS. Free money, right? Not so fast. A tax refund is your money that the IRS is returning to you. A tax refund means you've given the IRS a free loan of your money. Instead of planning to get a tax refund, how about if you plan to get a very small refund or better yet, none at all? You can probably make better use of the money now, rather than wait for a refund. If you regularly receive tax refunds, talk to a qualified tax expert to see what you can do to pay less in taxes today.

4 Smart Ways to Use Your Tax Refund

If for some reason you do get a large tax refund, here are some things you might consider doing with the extra cash:

1. Pay off debt – Using your tax refund to pay off credit card debt or student loan debt can jump that progress forward much faster than just paying the minimum monthly payment. Using your refund this way will also help decrease the amount of interest you pay, because you're

decreasing the balance by a large amount in a short period of time.

2. Fund Emergency Savings – Your tax refund is a great way to jump-start your emergency savings. We recommend that you have 3-6 months' worth of non-discretionary living expenses set aside for unexpected emergencies. With your tax refund as the base, be committed to then saving monthly until your emergency fund reaches the appropriate amount. And if you ever need to use your emergency savings, be diligent in replenishing it by again saving monthly until it returns to the original amount.

3. Set aside for a down payment – If you're planning on buying a home or a new car within the next year or so, set aside your tax refund in a savings account where it can then be used as a down payment toward a major purchase. It can be hard to save up large amounts of money for these types of purchases, so a tax refund is a great way to jump-start the savings.

4. Fund a Roth IRA – Since your tax refund is money that has already been taxed, it would make sense to then contribute this money to a Roth IRA (see the description above for more information on

this type of savings vehicle). Because the max contribution limit on Roth IRAs is $5,500 per year (as of 2018 and assuming you're under age 50 and you qualify), then your tax refund is again a great way to give you a jump start towards fully funding your Roth IRA for the year.

Chelsea Says:

Getting a tax refund can be exciting, until you realize that receiving a refund means you let the government borrow that money from you without having to pay any type of interest on it. If you don't receive a tax refund, and instead have to pay taxes on April 15, it's a hit to the pocketbook as well. Tax laws are constantly changing, so do what you can to stay up to date. What worked for you last year might not work this year. Also, don't take tax advice from your friends. Everyone's situation is different, and what worked for your friend may not be available to you. If, on April 15, you find yourself in an unexpected situation and owe more than you anticipated, it is wise to seek the advice of a CPA or qualified tax preparer. These people are up to date on new tax laws, and know what types of tax breaks are available to you. But don't wait until April. Find a CPA and make an appointment sometime in the Fall before they become booked full.

INVESTING

When we boil it down, YOU are the sole person responsible for your money. Whether you hire an investment advisor to help you invest, or a tax accountant to help you maximize your tax return, it's your money and you've got to take care of it.

The best way to take care of your money is to educate yourself. If you're reading this then good job! Take advantage of all the resources that are available like websites or podcasts. Some great books include "***Ditch the Guesswork: Creating Reliable ROI for Time Starved Investors***" by Steve Juetten, CFP®, and ***"I Will Teach You to Be Rich"*** by Ramit Sethi (both available on Amazon). Whatever way you prefer to consume information, it is out there for you.

*

A word of caution: ignore most of what you read in the popular press and hear on television and read on the web about investing. Most of it is financial garbage meant to separate you from your money by selling you things you don't need. See the section of this book on financial advisors to give you some ideas of who to listen to and who to ignore!

*

As you think about how you're going to invest your hard-earned dollars, it's a good idea to develop a **simple investing strategy** to guide you. As you create your investment approach, keep these five key principles in mind:

- Risk and return are related (there's no such thing as a free lunch).

- Spreading your dollar among different types of investments helps return (and helps you to sleep better at night!). For example, stocks and bonds act differently.

- No one can predict the future so buying the next "hot stock" because someone is hyping it is a waste of time and your dollars.

- Costs matter because every dollar you pay to a mutual fund company or advisor is a dollar out of your pocket.

- If it seems too good to be true, it probably is.

*

You often here terms thrown around the investing world like "stocks" and "bonds and 'mutual funds." One day a question occurred to us: "Does everyone know what these terms mean?" We decided that maybe not everyone does know what a stock is or what a bond is. So to help you, here are some basic descriptions.

First, what is a stock?

A share of stock is a share of ownership of a company. Corporations that are publically traded issue shares of ownership (or equity) that are then traded on exchanges like the New York Stock Exchange. By purchasing a share, you become an owner of the company. By becoming an owner, you are entitled to the corporation's assets and earnings. The benefit of becoming an owner is that, many companies reward their shareholders by distributing some of their earnings as dividends. Another way you can be rewarded by owning shares of a corporation is through the price of the share increasing due to increased demand. Of course companies also lose value or even go out of business, leaving little to nothing for the shareholders.

Because it is difficult if not impossible to consistently pick which stocks will rise in value, it's best to buy many stocks, and diversify your holdings. Never put all your eggs in one basket!

What Is a Mutual Fund?

The easiest way to diversify your holdings is through purchasing sharers of a mutual fund or its cousin, an Exchange Traded Fund (ETFs). Mutual funds and ETFs go out and buy a basket of stocks based on the goal of the fund. Mutual funds and ETFs own different types of stocks and bonds. Some own a basket of large U.S. companies, others own a basket of bonds and some specialize by owing real estate, global stocks and even commodities and natural resources.

What is a bond?

A bond is an I Owe You (with interest). Companies (and cities, governments, school districts) issue bonds as a way to borrow money.

When you purchase a bond, you are lending the company money with the expectation that they will pay you interest and when the bond matures, you'll also be paid back the original amount you lent the company. How much a bond pays in interest is known as a coupon payment.

For example, if my company *Kyle Style* wanted to borrow money from the public, it could issue 10 $1,000 dollar bonds and offer to pay 5% interest with a maturity of five years. If you purchased 5 units at issuing you would pay $5,000 dollars and receive $125 every six months until the bond matured in five years, when you would then receive your $5,000 back.

Of course just like a stock, the price of a bond changes based on supply and demand. So even though the original price of the bond might be $1,000, it could go down or up in value. As a bond nears its maturity date, the price gets closer to the original price.

I like to think of stocks and bonds as the ultimate side gig. I take on some risk with investing in them, but I'm also rewarded by investing in them.

Additionally, if you are investing in index funds you have to do a lot less work than trying to pick winners from losers. When deciding what to invest in, it's important to understand your risk tolerance, investment objective and time horizon.

*

When it comes to investing, one of the principles we value is being in it for the long-term. For you as an investor this means that once you invest your money, you shouldn't plan on selling it for at least 20+ years. But even if you are committed to this, you may not realize that the funds you are invested in may not be managed with the long-term in mind. Some funds may buy and sell investments frequently (essentially using your money to do so). The way you can measure how frequently a fund buys and sells is with the fund's turnover rate. If the turnover rate of a fund is 100%, this means that the fund replaces all its holdings within a 12 month period. If a fund you're invested in has a high turnover rate (anything above 25%) you may want to consider how this will impact you as a long-term investor. You may lose out on long-term gains, incur more fees, and may have to pay capital gains taxes sooner than you would like.

*

There are many savings vehicles that can be used to invest your money for your Financial Freedom Day. You have probably heard of traditional IRAs, Roth IRAs, 401(k)s, 403(b)s, and the list goes on. But, do you actually know what these accounts are or how they are different from each other?

The first place to start is always with the savings plan your employer offers. This is usually a 401(k) or 403(b) plan. These funny sounding names come from the IRS code sections that allow your employer to set up one of these plans for its employees. Many employers offer to match some of what you save and if you are lucky enough to have an employer who matches what you save this is key: **it's free money! Do not pass up the chance for free money ever.**

Even if your employer does not match your contributions, at least sign up for your employer savings plan as soon as you are eligible. The money comes out of your paycheck automatically before it's taxed.

*

If you are participating in your employer savings plan, like a 401(k) or 403(b) plan, you'll have some choices on how to invest your contributions and any company matching dollars. At first, it may look intimidating to decide how to invest your money, but these tips will help you to feel confident in making the right investment choices for yourself.

1. Many employer plans offer something called a **"target date fund."** Target Date funds are a simple way to invest, with minimal effort on your part. They typically have a year in their name, which should correspond to the year of your Financial Freedom Day. If you're 30, and want to be financially free when you're 65, then you want to choose the target date fund 35 years from now, 2052. A target date fund has a variety of different investments all within one fund. For example, a target date fund might have large and small U.S. stocks, non-U.S. stocks and bonds within it. This gives you instant diversification.

2. Another option is to invest among different mutual funds based on your risk tolerance. The 401(k)-plan provider may offer you a risk tolerance quiz. Take the quiz. Typically, the longer you have until your Financial Freedom Day, the more risk you can handle. This may be called "Aggressive." If you have a shorter time frame, you would be considered more

"Conservative." More aggressive investors typically have more stocks in their portfolio and less aggressive investors have more bonds.

3. If you go the individual mutual fund route, it's important to diversify among funds that invest in different kinds of stocks and bonds. Don't pick three mutual funds that all invest in the same thing; for example, choosing three mutual funds that all buy large U.S. stocks is not diversification. Instead, you could choose one fund that buys large U.S. stocks, one that buys small U.S. stocks, one that buys non-U.S. stocks and one that buys bonds. That would be better diversification.

4. It's also important to look at the fees charged by the mutual fund you choose. This fee is represented by the expense ratio of the fund. Some fund fees can go as high as 1%. Higher expense ratios eat into your earnings. There are great funds that invest in the same type of stocks or bonds with much lower expenses. Take the time to do a little shopping around to find a fund that fits your needs with low fees.

*

It's easy to assume that if someone is successful it's because they must have put in a lot of hard work to get there. But, oftentimes it's mostly due to luck. For example, say we had a stadium filled with 10,000 people and they each had a coin. We say that they will flip a coin once, and heads are winners and remain in the game, and tails are losers who are out. After round one we'd have about 5,000 people remaining, after round two we'd have about 2,500 people still in the game. After round three, about 1,250 people. Continuing on, after ten rounds we'd have about ten people left. Would you say that these people are expert coin flippers? No. You'd say they were just lucky. This luck comes from randomness.

The same can be said for someone who claims to be an expert investment manager who can pick the stocks that will be winners and help you consistently achieve above average returns. If they have picked winners in the past it was mainly due to luck and at some point their luck will run out. Keep this in mind if you're tempted to give your money to an investment manager who tries to convince you that they're a superior stock picker (coin flipper). Or if you're tempted to try your luck at picking stocks.

When it comes to investing, most people are concerned with what their return will be. So what if I told you that you yourself could increase your return by up to 39%? You'd probably say that's impossible, but it's not. The major factors that can decrease your return are the investment fees and expenses that you pay each year. The book, "Common Sense on Mutual Funds" by John Bogle gives an eye-opening example. If you pay a one percent fee, it will reduce your ending account balance by 17 percent over a ten year period. A two percent fee would reduce the account balance by 24 percent over a ten year period and 39 percent over a 25 year period (dependent upon the actual rate of return). So inversely, this means that if you can decrease your fees you will be increasing your returns.

Whether it's your IRA, 401(k), or just a regular brokerage account, fees can eat away at any return you might be getting. Take a look at your next account statement and see how much you're paying in fees each month, or annually. If you see fees above 1%, you may want to consider looking into other low cost investment options (ideally less than .5%). To rephrase a common saying, "You get what you don't pay for."

*

Here's an example of the value of saving a little every year. If you opened a Traditional IRA when you were 25 and:

- Saved $5,500 each year, and

- Your account earned 6% on average each year,

You would have $301,755 in your Traditional IRA account at age 50.

The bottom line: save a little regularly.

Chelsea Says:

I recently read a very interesting piece of information from Burton Malkiel's book, "A Random Walk Down Wall Street". In the book, Malkiel explains that if you had invested $1 in the Dow Jones Industrial Average (an index of 30 major U.S. stocks) in 1900, by the start of 2013 it would have grown to $290. Even more interesting is that if you had missed out on the best five days of each year during that time period, that same $1 would have been worth less than a penny in 2013.

This just goes to show that being out of the market for even just a few days each year can have a dramatic impact on your returns. That's why when investing in the stock market, you've got to be in it for the long-run and not try to time when to get in or out of your investments. It's like planting a tree and watching it grow – you wouldn't run out and pull it up every time it rains or snows or the wind blows hard would you?

Chelsea Says:

When I first began investing, it was in a Roth IRA. I opened one up after starting my job as a financial planner. I was disappointed to find out that I could not invest my first $50 contribution. To my dismay, most mutual funds require a $1000 minimum to buy in. Sure, I could have bought $50 of XYZ stock, but that wasn't my plan. So, if you're like me and have to start out small, don't let it deter you. Slowly build up that cash amount each month until you've got enough to invest in a fund. Ideally, with small amounts like $1000, you can choose a target date fund that corresponds to the year you would like to retire. Target date funds are a great way to diversify small amounts of money. For example a Target Date Fund 2035 means that you'd like to retire in the year 2035

The fund will hold appropriate amounts of stocks and bonds, and shift these amounts to be more conservative as it gets closer to that year. As your account size grows, you can then leave the fund and invest in more diversified investment options if you prefer.

Additional Resources

Considering opening an IRA? Here's a great article that will help calm your nerves and walk you through the steps to get started.
http://www.bankrate.com/finance/investing/ira-investing-for-beginners-1.aspx

EMPLOYEE BENEFITS

Companies that offer employee benefits have an annual Open Enrollment period. During this time period (often in October or November), you can make changes to your benefits, add or delete coverage. Usually, the only time during the year that you can change your benefit elections is during this open enrollment period. Note: if you have a change in your family status due to a major qualifying event (marriage, divorce, birth, death or adoption) during the year, you can change your benefits then.

For example, during open enrollment you could change your health care insurance coverage or change the amount of disability income coverage. The open enrollment period is a good time to review your medical expenses from the past year to determine whether you are purchasing the appropriate coverage. You can also consider if a Healthcare Spending Account (HCSA) or a Dependent Care Spending Account (DCSA) is a good idea for you if your employer offers them (we discuss these types of plans more below) Open enrollment is a great time to think ahead and plan for your future.

Many companies also introduce changes to the benefits they provide during the open enrollment period. While you may not think that much has changed in your life, and that you do not need to make changes to your elected benefits, it is worth looking through the information to understand any changes to benefits for the coming year. Employee benefits offered by your employer can increase your total pay by up to 30%. This is why it's important to sit down and look through the benefits information during open enrollment and make sure that you are optimizing what is available.

During your company's open enrollment you will probably be sent, either through regular mail or email, a large packet of information on your company's employee benefits. As we mentioned, it is important to read over this information to ensure that you are optimizing the benefits available to you. Reading through all this information can be tedious and overwhelming. In order for you to make sound choices about the benefits you elect to receive, it's important that you understand the terminology used. We've compiled a list of terms that will help you better understand the benefits being offered to you.

*

Benefit Plan Terms

Here are some terms you might need to know when it comes to your benefits at work:

Deductible – The dollar amounts you're responsible for paying before your insurance plan begins paying

Coinsurance – Your share of the cost of a service, usually a percentage, after you've paid the deductible

Copayment – a fixed dollar amount that an insured must pay for a covered medical service

Out of Pocket Maximum – the maximum amount you pay out of pocket for services during a one-year period

Elimination Period – also called waiting period, the time required to pass before you're eligible to receive benefits

Any Occupation – a strict definition of disability that requires a person to be so severely disabled that he or she cannot engage in any occupation

Beneficiary – the person designated to receive the proceeds of a life insurance policy, also the person designated to receive any retirement accounts should the account owner die

Buy-up plan – also called a supplemental plan, an employee benefit plan under which a covered person can purchase additional coverage (for example, life insurance or disability income insurance) at his or her own expense

Cafeteria plan – an employee benefit plan through which an employee can use a specified amount of employer funds and/or salary reductions to design his or her own benefit package from an array of available benefits

Family Deductible – a provision in a medical plan that waives future deductibles for all family members once a specified total dollar amount of medical expenses has been incurred or after a specified number of family members have satisfied their individual deductibles

Health Maintenance Organization (HMO) – a managed system of health care that provides a comprehensive array of medical services on a prepaid basis to enrolled persons living within a specific geographic region. HMOs both finance health care and deliver health services and there is an emphasis on preventive care as well as cost control.

Portability – the ability to continue employer-provided or employer-sponsored benefits after termination of employment

Preferred Provider Organization (PPO) – a group of health care providers that contract with employers or others to provide medical care services at a reduced fee

*

Flexible Spending Account

You may have heard of an employee benefit called a **Flexible Spending Account (FSA).** There are two types of Flexible Spending Accounts – one for health care expenses and another type for dependent care expenses.

But what exactly is a Flexible Spending Account and why should you care? Before you decide to open an FSA because you heard a coworker say that they were opening one, let's look at the purpose and details of an FSA.

A Flexible Spending Account is an account where you can deposit before-tax dollars to use toward certain employee selected benefits. A health care FSA can be used to pay medical expenses other than insurance premiums. These expenses can include medical or dental expenses not covered by the insurance plan, like deductibles and copayments. A dependent care FSA can be used to pay dependent care expenses, such as monthly day care costs.

The advantage of any FSA is that expenses are paid with pre-tax dollars. The major disadvantage to an FSA is that the money in the account must be used by the end of the year or it will be forfeited, often referred to as "use it or lose it." So before you decide to have money pulled from your paychecks and deposited into an FSA, be sure that you carefully estimate the costs to which you plan on using this money. Overestimating could cause you to forfeit any money left in the account at the end of the year.

Health Savings Account (HSA)

Your employer may offer a plan called a Health Savings Plan or HSA. An HSA is different from a health care spending account (FSA) because unlike an FSA, any money deposited in an HSA does not have the "use it or lose it" rule. Money in an HSA is deposited without being taxed and as long as it is used for qualified medical expenses, the money is not taxed when it's withdrawn. Another feature and benefit of an HSA is that the money is held in an account and can be deposited into an investment account and thereby earn returns so the account grows. Think of an HSA as a health care 401(K) plan.

Most often you will see an HSA attached to a high-deductible medical plan. If your employer offers an HSA option to you, carefully consider it because it can be a good vehicle to save for future medical expenses. However, a Health Savings Account can be tricky so be sure you understand how to use it before you sign up for it.

*

Benefits That Pay You When You Can't Work

One benefit that some companies offer is disability income coverage. Did you know that during the course of your career, you are three and a half times more likely to be injured and need disability benefits than you are to die and need life insurance benefits? Whether you're single or married, with kids or without, you need disability insurance to protect your income.

There are different types of disability coverages based on the different definitions of "totally disabled". There is "any occupation" disability insurance, which means you must be so disabled that you are prevented from performing the duties of any occupation for which you are reasonably suited by education, training, and experience. Then there is "own occupation" disability insurance, which means you are considered totally disabled if you are unable to perform the duties of your regular occupation at the time of disability.

For example, under the own occupation definition, if a surgeon injures her hand so badly while skiing that she can no longer perform surgeries, then disability insurance would pay a benefit. Even if the surgeon could be a teacher, her disability coverage would still pay disability benefits because she could no longer perform surgeries. There are also other modified definitions of disabled, so be sure to read the definitions in your plan carefully.

Here is a way to think about the importance of disability benefits. If you are sick or injured and can't work, you will still need to buy food, pay your rent, and meet your other obligations. If that happened to you, would you be able to meet your financial obligations? If disability insurance is an option offered to you through your employer, we recommend that you sign up for coverage, and if possible, increase the benefits to pay at least 2/3 of your income if you're sick or injured and can't work.

*

Life Insurance

Ugh. Who wants to read about or even think about life insurance? If you're single, you might not care. But if you're married – and especially if you have kids – then life insurance is definitely something to think about.

We like to describe life insurance as "income interruption insurance". If you're married and are the sole bread winner for your family, or if your family relies on two incomes, having life insurance coverage on the income earners ensures that if one of the income earners of the family dies unexpectedly, then income that the family would have relied on from that person would still be received through life insurance coverage.

You can get life insurance from two sources: your employer or a private company. Life insurance through your employer is typically offered in amounts tied to your salary. For example, you may purchase life insurance coverage with a benefit of 1.5 times your salary. Buying a private policy means you can buy any amount you want, although it is usually purchased in $100,000 or even $250,000 increments. While the cost to buy insurance through your work is usually the least expensive way to purchase insurance, you may be limited to the amount of coverage that you can purchase. Something to keep in mind is that this insurance coverage is only available while you are an employee of that company. If you decide to leave your job or are terminated, you will no longer be covered.

To calculate how much life insurance coverage you need, try these online calculators.
Visit **www.lifehappens.org** or **www.bankrate.com** for these calculators.

*

401(k) & 403(b) Savings Plans

One of the most common employee benefit plans is a 401(k) or 403(b) employer savings plan. A 401(k) or 403(B) plan is a retirement savings vehicle provided by an employer. This type of plan allows you to contribute pre-tax dollars towards your retirement savings. The money grows tax-free as well (until you take it out). Distributions from your 401(k) or 403(b) plan are taxed as ordinary income at whichever tax bracket you fall into during that year. And you may pay a penalty if you try to take out money before you're 60 years old.

If your company offers a matching contribution, try to maximize your contributions to receive all the matching that is available to you.

For example, if your company matches 50% of your contribution up to 6% of your pay, then if you contribute 6% of your pay, your company will contribute 3% for a total contribution of 9%. It's like getting free money!

If you can't put in enough to get the maximum matching contributions, start by saving a small amount each paycheck ($50/paycheck) and try to increase your contributions by 1% each year until you reach that maximum matching amount. Some companies offer automatic escalation, which will increase the amount for you each year. If your company offers this feature, sign up for it. You won't miss the extra money from your paycheck and before you know it, you'll be saving close to the target savings amount we suggest (at least 10% of your pay and preferably 15%).

Once you've joined your 401(k) or 403(b) plan and are contributing, you need to know how your money is being invested. Many companies offer **target date** funds. These funds are invested according to the year that you plan on retiring. For example, if you're 28 right now and plan on retiring at 66, you would invest in a target date fund which would probably be labeled with the year you plan on retiring, for example, Target Date Fund 2055. These funds slowly transition from being more heavily weighted in stocks to being more weighted in bonds.

This allows for earnings growth while you're young and have time, and transitions to protecting and preserving your money through investing in bonds.

*

Company Stock

You've just signed your employment contract and are now wondering about the details of your benefits. You know that a portion of your pay will be received in company stock that vests over time (vesting means you gain ownership of the stock over time; for example, stock might vest 25% each year over four years). You may even be in a position that qualifies for performance stock awards. This may be pretty confusing so we'll cover various forms of equity or stock compensation that may be part of your total pay package in the next few tips.

First, these are the typical types of equity or stock compensation:

- Non-Qualified Stock Options (NSO's)
- Incentive Stock Options
- Restricted Stock Units and Awards
- Performance Stock Units
- Special Mentions: ESOP and ESPP

*

NSO's

Non-Qualified Stock Options (NSO's) are shares of company stock that are granted as part of your total pay. The granted stock is not given without a cost to you though. NSO's have an "exercise price", or a price that you have to pay each share. Also the shares sometimes become available or vest after a certain amount of time has passed. Once vested you have the option to buy the shares at the exercise price, which is hopefully lower than the current price. After exercise, you can either hold the shares, sell them immediately or sell them in the future.

The advantages of NSO's are:

1. **Access to company shares at a known exercise price**; which ideally would be much lower than the market price.

2. **Potential deferral of gains** because you can choose when to sell the shares.

3. It may also **encourage you to work harder and help improve the success of your company** because you have "skin in the game."

The disadvantage of NSO's is that it's not guaranteed that the company share prices will exceed the exercise price.

Obviously you wouldn't sell stock if the market price was less than the price of the stock when it was granted to you, but if NSO's are part of your compensation package, then there is an element of risk.

Another disadvantage with company stock is the lack of diversification owning company stock presents. Think of it this way: your paycheck and investments are tied to one entity (your company). That's not much diversification. If the company fails, you could lose both your job and the value of the stock. Also there are some tax implications when exercising and selling NSO's that go beyond the scope of this tip so make sure you check with a qualified tax expert before you sell any NSO's. Just know that there is no free lunch!

There are three ways to exercise a NSO's.

1. A cash exercise is the simplest method; you come up with the cash to purchase the shares at the exercise price. This may require a large outlay of cash, depending on the exercise price and quantity of shares that you exercise. Quite often

though, you may not have the cash on hand, in which case the cashless exercise may be used.

2. In a cashless exercise, the funds needed to exercise are loaned to you by the company and after the transaction, are repaid with proceeds from the exercise.

3. The last method is a stock swap, where you would sell some shares to cover the exercise.

*

ISO's

Not as common as in prior years, ISO's are similar to NSO's, however, the bargain element (the spread between the exercise price and market price) is treated as a long term capital gain. Additionally, there are restrictions around ISO's: to qualify for the long term gains, the shares must be held two years from date of grant and one year from date of exercise. Options may also not last longer than ten years and the maximum exercisable amount in one year is $100,000. The bargain element is also subject to Alternative Minimum Tax (AMT) as a preference item.

If you have access to ISO's, you will want to work with a CPA to minimize any tax events. The advantages of ISO's are similar to NSO's, however, the bargain element is considered a capital gain, and not taxed as W2 income. Usually, a capital gain is taxed at a lower rate than your income tax rate so that's good. The disadvantage is that in order to qualify for the favorable capital gains treatment, you have to meet the required holding periods. This presents a risk that the shares fall in price over the intervening years. Additionally, ISO's may complicate your taxes due to the AMT preference.

*

Restricted Stock Units (RSU's) and Awards (RSA's)

RSU's and RSA's are the most common form of stock compensation with tech companies and startups. They provide an incentive for employees to stay by using vesting schedules and to work hard by linking your total compensation to a company's share price. In some cases, a performance requirement may have to be met in order to receive the stock. Granted shares are treated as W2 income at the market price on the vesting date.

Unlike NSO's and ISO's, there is no exercise price built into the grant. Restricted Stock Units will always be worth something (unless the company goes under).

A disadvantage of RSU's and RSA's are their vesting schedules. You may find yourself in a job you'd rather not be in, but because you are waiting for an RSU to vest, you may feel tied to the position. One distinction between RSU's and RSA's is known as an 83(b) election. RSA's allow you to pay regular income tax on the **grant date**, instead of the **vest date**. This is a good decision if you expect the share price to be higher at the vest date. However, if the share price is less, you do not recover any of the taxes paid. Additionally, you only have 30 days from the grant date to make the decision to file for an 83(b) election.

*

Performance Stock Units/Awards (PSU's and PSA's)

Similar to RSA's and RSU's, PSU's and PSA's are stock grants that are tied to performance measures.

The amount received is tied to company or group goals that have to be met. These types of stock compensation still vest over time and are taxed in a similar manner to RSU's.

A Note on Tax Planning: tax issues on any type of stock compensation are complex. Be sure to consult with a qualified tax expert so you understand the ins and outs of how stock compensation is handled from a tax standpoint.

*

ESPP and ESOPs

An Employee Stock Purchase Plans (ESPP) gives you the option to purchase your employer's stock at a grant price that is no more than 15% below the market value on the grant date or exercise date. Like ISO's the shares must be held for at least two years from grant, and one year from the date of exercise. Additionally, employees are limited to $25,000 a year in ESPP grants. Here are some advantages to an ESPP:

- You buy company stock at a discount. You're guaranteed a gain.

- It's easy. You can contribute automatically through payroll deductions, just like with your 401(k).

- It's another way to save for your financial freedom day.

- You can be an owner of your company and only have to invest a small amount each month. Many ESPP's require only $10 or $15 per paycheck to participate.

- Your savings in an ESOP are more accessible than savings within a 401(k). Although taxes may still apply, you can withdraw the money from an ESOP without the penalties and/or repayment requirements that apply when you take a loan or withdrawal from a 401(k) account. This means you can use ESOP funds for a variety of goals like a down payment for a home, to make extra payments on student loans or any other "life" expenses.

In an **Employee Stock Ownership Plan** (ESOP), a company puts shares of company stock into a special account and then divides up those shares among employees based on a formula. The contributions are deductible for the employer and are taxed to the employee when withdrawn (usually at retirement or on leaving employment). An employee can continue deferring taxes since shares can be rolled over into an IRA. Similar to the other forms of equity compensation, a disadvantage of ESOP's is the lack of diversification that occurs from owning a large amount of shares from one company.

FINDING A FINANCIAL PLANNER

When you think of a financial planner, you probably think of someone who picks stocks, watches a computer screen, and tells people when to buy and sell stocks throughout the day. That person is an ***investment manager***, not a financial planner. In reality, financial planners do much more than just watch the stock market.

Financial planners look at all aspects of your financial life including your cash flow, how you're managing your debts, education planning, retirement planning, insurance, tax planning, estate planning and, yes, even your investments. A true financial planner looks at your current situation and your goals and helps you determine how all these pieces can fit together in the best, most effective way possible for you.

A good financial planner will keep you on track when times get tough. He or she will ease your fears and ensure that you are making rational, well thought out decisions, and will help you to adjust your plan as your goals and needs change as you go through life.

*

When choosing a financial advisor, it's important to know all the different ways that financial advisors get paid. If you can determine how an advisor is paid, then you will know what conflicts of interest an advisor has as they give you advice. Make no mistake-- most advisors will sell you the services or products that favor **_them_** the most. The four main ways that advisors get paid are:

1. **Commission Only** – This type of advisor receives commissions when they sell certain investments, insurance, or bonds to their clients. An example would be a broker working at Merrill Lynch, who may receive a commission based on what investment they sell you. Also, this type of financial advisor does not have to tell to you that they are getting paid a commission to sell you this product, even if you ask.

2. **Commission and Fees** – In addition to receiving commissions for selling certain products, this type of advisor will also receive fees for providing additional services. Oftentimes, the advisor will receive a fee for creating the financial plan, and then receive a commission for selling the investment products once the plan is implemented. This is also called "fee-based."

3. **Salary and Bonus** – Employees of the big brokerage firms like Vanguard, Fidelity, Charles Schwab, etc. are usually paid a salary for their daily work, and receive bonuses for bringing in new clients or selling certain products, for example a specific mutual fund or insurance product.

4. **Fee-Only** – A fee-only advisor is paid purely to give you advice and receives no other compensation by working with you. Usually, these advisors have their own Registered Investment Advisor (RIA) company or they work for one.

Understanding how your financial advisor gets paid is important because it helps you understand where your money is going, and more specifically what services you are actually paying for (or paying extra for!). Keep in mind that some financial advisors do not have to tell you how they get paid, or whether they are making a commission by selling you XYZ product. This directly relates to the trust that you could have with your advisor, and what obligations the advisor owes to you.

*

Always choose a financial advisor that is a "**fiduciary**." Why? Because advisors that are fiduciaries must legally put their clients' interests first before their own. Again, you'd probably expect this from anyone that calls him or herself a "financial advisor", "financial planner", "investment manager", "wealth manager" etc. but that's not the case. Financial advisors that are **not** fiduciaries are only required to give advice that is "suitable." This means that the non-fiduciary advisor legally can knowingly give you advice that is not the best advice for you, as long as it is suitable to you.

Non-fiduciary advisors must put their **company's interests before** your interests, which can lead to conflicts of interest.

With a fee-only financial advisor, you're purely paying for their advice. With any other type of financial advisor, the line is blurred between paying for advice versus paying for the product they are selling. And, choosing an advisor who owes you fiduciary duties will always give you the confidence that your advisor has your best interests first when creating a financial plan or giving you financial advice.

Please note: all the advisors with the **Financial Foundations Program** and Juetten Personal Financial Planning, LLC are fiduciaries. Always have been. Visit us at **www.takecareofyourmoney.com** or check out the website of Juetten Personal Financial Planning, LLC at **www.finpath.com**.

*

If you're in a situation where you need advice about money, who should you listen to? Do you ask your parents? Clearly they would never steer you in the wrong direction, right? Do you ask your friends?

Sometimes parents give unrealistic guidance, so friends that you trust might be able to relate to you and give you practical advice, right? Wrong.

While they may have good intentions, parents and friends don't always have the right information. They can be mistaken about the details and could give advice that has unintended negative consequences. Also, it's important to understand that what worked for your parents or a friend may not be the best advice for you.

Each person has different goals and different financial situations, so when seeking financial advice it's important to talk to a **fee-only** and holistic financial planner who will take your complete situation into account before making any specific suggestions.

Chelsea Says:

When I first started looking for a job as a financial planner, I knew that I did not want to be someone who got paid on a commission. How could someone trust me knowing that I was getting paid to sell them something? It just didn't feel right. I knew that I wanted to be a fee-only financial planner, someone that is paid to give advice. So, when you're searching for a financial planner, be aware of the different ways a financial planner can get paid, commissions, fee-based, fee-only, etc. It's acceptable to ask questions about how they get paid because it's an important part of the planner-client relationship. If you don't trust that you're being charged fairly, then it will be hard for you to trust any advice or recommendations from the planner as well. I may be biased towards fee-only planners, but there are plenty of great planners who charge in different ways. Just be sure you choose a planner that you feel you can trust.

Additional Resources

Take a look at this article and once you've read it, you'll feel much more confident about how to choose a financial advisor that meets your financial advising needs. **http://twocents.lifehacker.com/how-to-find-and-hire-a-financial-advisor-who-won-t-rip-1729724424**

ESTATE PLANNING

Estate Planning – ugh. You might think this topic is for old people, but we all need to plan for what will happen after we die. Unfortunately (or fortunately?), none of us know when this will happen so it's important to have a plan. When there is a plan in place, it makes it much easier for your surviving relatives as it is one less thing for them to have to worry about during such a distressing time.

When we talk about Estate Planning, there are four main legal documents we're talking about. The first of these is a **will**, which lets your estate executor (the person who will carry out your instructions) know how you'd like your assets to be distributed after you've passed. If you do not have a will, your assets will be distributed according to the laws of the state you live in. These laws may not distribute your assets the way you'd want, so it's important to have a will so that things can be done the way you want.

The next is the **Durable Power of Attorney for Health Care**, which gives the person named the power to act on your behalf in medical matters even if you are incapacitated. This means they have the power to make medical decisions for you. This agent would carry out your wishes on medical care and treatment preferences, which are written out in the next estate plan document called a **living will**. Note: some states call this an **Advance Directive** or **Directive to Physicians**. They all have the same purpose. The living will provides end of life directions to the agent and health care providers to follow

Finally, there is the **General Durable Power of Attorney for Finances**. The holder of this power can make financial decisions on your behalf. You can also give this person as little or as much power over your finances as you'd like. You could allow them to do only small things, like deposit checks into your bank account or collect your mail. Or you could allow them to do things like invest your money or even buy and sell real estate on your behalf.

Regardless of whether you're single with no kids, married or have kids, these documents are important for everyone. They can be simple documents, or they can be complex depending on your specific situation. This is a part of comprehensive financial planning that often gets overlooked. It's not glamorous, and it can sometimes make people feel uncomfortable to think about incapacitation or death. But it is just as important as all the other pieces that make up the comprehensive financial planning puzzle.

The purpose of Estate Planning, and all the documents that go along with it, is to ensure that your family is taken care of the way YOU want them to be. Without the right estate planning documents, everything is left up to the state to decide for you. In addition, when left up to the state, things can take a very long time to be processed through the courts. When you have everything planned, the process is much smoother and quicker and saves your surviving family members from having to make these decisions or worry about what the court might decide.

If you have not thought about estate planning, now is the time to get started.

*

One aspect of estate planning that is often overlooked is the importance of getting your personal financial information collected and organized in case there is a bump along the road of life like disability, divorce or death. The **Life Goes on Roadmap**™ system for personal financial information organization offers the tools, resources, and accountability to get this done.

Life Goes on Roadmap™ is an affordable and empowering toolkit to organize personal finance information for today's digital age so you and your family members have power, access, and control, before disease, disability or death get in the way. Users are more confident about their personal financials when they organize important contacts, service providers, insurance information, bank or credit union accounts, investments, credit cards, and more so the information is accessible when and where it is needed. Life Goes on Roadmap elevates the process of getting organized to be a game to win instead of an administrative task to put off until later. Visit **www.authenticvisibility.com/roadmap** to learn more and make your wise purchase or refer this link to parents, family members, and friends who can benefit right now.

*

We've talked with some estate planning attorneys about the best way to complete estate planning documents all of them said that the best thing to do is to see an estate planning attorney to have your estate documents prepared, rather than using online services or estate planning software. We understand that you may be early in your professional career and therefore you may think that you don't have the money to pay an attorney. It may be tempting to go with the least expensive option like do-it-yourself software, but it really is best to have a professional help you. Here's why:

The estate attorneys we talked to all mentioned that using an estate planning attorney will help you cover all the bases. "The issue is that people don't need a 'document'. They need the counsel in order to have a 'document' that will do what they want it to do and not lead to unintended consequences," says attorney Brita Long. The attorney provides you personalized advice for your specific circumstances so that your affairs are handled the way you would like. This advice is something that online services and software cannot provide you. Using online legal services or software may be less expensive, but it may also leave you exposed to problems, as you may be unaware of certain laws or rules and not cover them appropriately when you prepare your estate documents yourself.

*

If you decide to start looking for an estate planning attorney, look for one that will charge you a flat fee. If your situation is fairly straightforward, a flat fee should be the most economical way for you to get your estate planning documents completed by an attorney. You will know how much it is going to cost going into it, and there will be no surprises when you receive the bill. The alternative to a flat fee is to pay an attorney by the hour, which could lead to you paying more than you expect.

*

Now that you know how important it is to have your estate planning documents prepared by an attorney, how do you find one? You could ask friends, family members or someone you trust like a CPA or financial planner. Or you could check with your local county bar association. They should have a list of estate planning attorneys in your area. Call a few attorneys and see if any charge a flat fee for preparing estate documents, and compare a few prices.

This link also has some other good suggestions as to how to find an estate planning attorney.
https://www.thebalance.com/finding-estate-planning-attorney-3505704

*

Estate planning rules are state law driven. This means that the laws about estate planning and estate tax are different in each state. For example, in California, if you die without a will, the estate attorney assigned to your case automatically receives a fee of 10% of your estate's value. To avoid this, people in California can create a living trust which minimizes the size of their estate and therefore minimizes the fee they pay the attorney. This recommendation may be appropriate for people living in California but may not be appropriate for people living in Nebraska because the laws are different.

*

Thinking about what happens if you die is critical when you have kids. It is in your will where you designate who will be the guardian(s) of your children should you die while they are minors. Having a will for this purpose is important because if there is no will, a judge will appoint guardians to look after your children with the best interests of the child(ren) in mind. This process could take a long time and it's even possible that a child would be placed in foster care until a guardian is appointed.

When you have kids, it is also important to keep in mind who you have listed as your beneficiary for things like 401(k) plans, life insurance plans, and other investment accounts. It is important to always revisit these accounts and update the beneficiaries when major life milestones, like having children, occur. You may find that the person you had listed when you first opened the account may now not be who you want as your beneficiary.

*

You may also want to consider making your bank accounts, like checking and savings accounts, Payable on Death (POD) or Transfer on Death (TOD) accounts. This can be done to any existing bank account and in some cases even your investment accounts (although not IRA or Roth IRA accounts). A POD or TOD allows the account and all the money in it to be directly transferred to the beneficiary you list. If you are married, your spouse can keep their rights to the bank account and the account can be Payable on Death to the listed beneficiary after the second spouse passes away. A Payable on Death bank account avoids any Estate Taxes, so all the money goes straight to the beneficiary.

*

Any assets, like money from your bank account, or money from your 401(k), that your under-age child inherits must be placed into a trust. There are many types of trusts that can distribute the assets within the trust in many different ways. The trust must have a trustee, who is the person in charge of the trust and how the assets are handled. The trustee is usually a trusted adult that will be responsible for the trust until the child becomes an adult. Or the trustee may be a bank or trust company. The child who has rights to the assets within the trust is considered the beneficiary. Some trusts might distribute a specific amount of money to the child's guardian every month, while other trusts might stipulate that the beneficiary cannot receive the trust assets until a specific point in time, like when they turn 18 or graduate college.

Trusts can be complex and this article does a good job of explaining them, how they work, and how nearly anyone can create a trust.

https://www.investopedia.com/articles/pf/12/set-up-a-trust-fund.asp

---

Chelsea Says:

When I started working as a financial planner, it became very apparent that being married with children necessitates having a will, Powers of Attorney, and advanced medical directive. If something were to happen to me, or my husband, or both of us, these important pieces of paper would ensure that our wishes and desires for our family were followed.

I can relate to feeling like taking the time to find an attorney and sit down and do the paperwork seems like an absolute chore. But once you've completed your estate documents, you will feel a huge weight lifted off of your shoulder. And in the end, we all hope they are papers we will never need, but will be grateful that they exist if we unfortunately ever come to need them.

WHY FREEZING YOUR CREDIT IS NOW EASIER THAN EVER

By Amy Shappell, CFP®
Senior Financial Planner
Juetten Personal Financial Planning, LLC

As a part of the Economic Growth, Regulatory Relief and Consumer Protection Act, fees for implementing and removing credit freezes at consumer reporting agencies were eliminated in September 2018. This means that protecting your credit history is getting simpler and less expensive.

What is a credit freeze?

A credit freeze is a way to protect your personal information from fraud and identity theft. Implementing a credit freeze means that no one can access your credit files to open a new account in your name.

Fees varied by state, but previously, it could cost up to $30 for consumers to freeze their credit reports with the three major credit bureaus, and the same fees applied to lift the freeze.

Credit bureaus offer a similar service called a credit 'lock'. However, there are some significant differences. Rules to freeze your credit are mandated by law. Credit locks are designed and implemented by each credit bureau and the rules vary. In addition, you may be subject to fees, your information may be used for marketing purposes or shared with other financial companies, and in the case of TransUnion, you are compelled to agree to an arbitration clause.

How to implement a credit freeze

You can freeze your credit file by calling or filling out a form on the website of each credit bureau. The three largest of these are:

Equifax: www.equifax.com/personal/credit-report-services/

Experian: www.experian.com/help

TransUnion: www.transunion.com/credit-help

You will need your name, address, date of birth, Social Security number and additional personal information to confirm your identity. When your credit is frozen, each credit bureau issues you a PIN to use to freeze and thaw your account. As with any password, it's important to keep this number confidential.

The freeze will remain in place until you ask the credit bureau to remove it, either temporarily or permanently. If the request is made online or by phone, action to lift the freeze must be made within an hour; if the request is made by mail, then the company must remove the freeze no later than three business days after receiving your letter. To apply for a loan or credit card, you will need to lift the freeze on your account. Applying for insurance or renting an apartment may also spur a credit check. A potential employer may check your credit as part of a job application. All of these will necessitate a temporary lift of the freeze.

Should you place a credit freeze?

While there is no longer a monetary cost to placing a freeze on your credit, there is still a cost in terms of the time and effort to contact each credit bureau.

However, the cost is minor in comparison to the time it might take to recover from identity theft. If you are in the midst of shopping for a mortgage or car loan, placing a credit freeze doesn't make sense. For most others, placing a credit freeze will offer some additional peace of mind.

We recommend that you check your credit at least annually via **www.annualcreditreport.com**. If you see fraudulent credit activity, then implementing a credit freeze is a must.

Keep in mind, however, that if your current credit information falls into the hands of a criminal as a result of a theft or data breach, a credit freeze won't prevent your card from being used to make fraudulent purchases. A credit freeze only prevents unauthorized persons from opening new accounts in your name.

Placing a credit freeze does not change your credit score. In addition, freezing your credit will not stop prescreened credit offers, and existing creditors and debt collectors acting on behalf of your existing creditors will still have access to your credit report.

Additional impacts of the new law

Fraud alerts. The new law also makes changes to fraud alerts. A fraud alert is a less stringent way to protect your credit. Instead of being prohibited from obtaining your credit report, when lenders pull your reports they will be notified that you may be the victim of identity theft and should reach out to you before opening an account in your name.

Previously, fraud alerts stayed in place 90 days; now the time on an initial alert is extended to one year and victims of identity theft can extend the fraud alert to seven years.

Protection for children. More than 1 million children were victims of identity theft in 2017. Children are particularly vulnerable because no records exist on them and the fraud can go undiscovered for years. Parents can now place a freeze on a credit file for children under 16. Often, children won't have a credit file, but the law directs the credit bureaus to create one and then freeze it, protecting the child from fraud. When placing a credit freeze on a child's account, be sure to secure the PIN used to thaw the account. Placing a credit freeze on your children's accounts is an easy way to safeguard their future credit.

Military personnel. Within a year, credit reporting agencies must offer free electronic credit monitoring to all active duty military.

A Final Thought

Building a solid credit history is an important part of your financial life. The ability to freeze and thaw your credit record for free means that there is one less barrier to being able to protect your credit history, giving you a simpler way to keep your personal information safe. Take advantage of the opportunity.

ALTERNATIVE FINANCE

There's a growing group of mostly younger people who are taking a different approach to their careers. This group is following an approach called FIRE – Financial Independence Retire Early. The group has a different philosophy to personal finance in that they typically save more than 60% of their income AND sometimes as much as 80%. This means that they keep their expenses extremely low and their income as high as possible. They may sacrifice things like owning a car and choose to walk or ride a bike everywhere, or they may give up owning a pet so that they can avoid spending any money unnecessarily. Or they control expenses in combination with high paying, but low satisfaction jobs and work like crazy for a few years. By saving most of their income, they are able to build up the amount needed to become financially independent very quickly. Depending on the savings amount, an individual could retire in as little as five to ten years. Once the goal amount is saved, someone who adheres to the FIRE methodology is able to retire early and live off the interest that their money is making.

The point of reaching FIRE is different for each person. Much like any other personal financial goal, it is based on the individual's personal goals and financial situation. The big picture is that you make sacrifices now so that you can achieve and enjoy your dream life in the future.

Chelsea Says:

If you think the FIRE method might be a good idea, the next question is "What will you do once you reach financial independence?" I am fortunate enough to have had my husband retire early (not planned for but that's another story), and I choose to work in financial planning because I enjoy it, not because I have to put food on the table. He keeps busy by coaching a high school basketball team, as well as our son's baseball team. We do not live an extravagant life, we don't have shiny new cars, and our house is nice, but no McMansion. We keep our expenses low so that we can enjoy the things in life that are important to us. The FIRE method is a great way to help you reach that point in your life where you can do what makes you happy, but first you need to determine what it is that makes you happy before adopting drastic lifestyle change that FIRE requires.

DEALING WITH MONEY ANXIETY

A recent study by Fundrise found that 62.7% of young professionals do not feel prepared for the next financial crisis. And nearly half of those surveyed believe there is nothing they can do about it. Let us say that this is not true. There are steps you can take to prepare yourself for the next financial crisis.

When we say "financial crisis", we're talking about a sharp down-turn in the stock market or an economic bubble popping. These financial crises happen about every seven to ten years. Therefore, it's important to be prepared because it's not a matter of IF a financial crisis will happen, but WHEN.

The first way to become better prepared is to ensure that your investment portfolio is diversified throughout many asset classes, including stocks (large cap, mid cap, and small cap), bonds, real estate and even commodities. Each of these classes has different risks, and when you spread out your risk among many asset classes, your portfolio is considered diversified.

Finally, it's important to remember that you are in it for the long run. When a financial crisis occurs, it's important to keep your investments where they are, and not make any financial decisions based on fear. Those that stayed in the market after the 2007-2008 financial crisis made their money back in two to three years. Don't run away when a financial crisis occurs. Prepare your portfolio and know that when a financial crisis happens, you're ready to weather the storm.

*

In addition to a major down-turn in the investment markets, there are other events that could be a financial crisis for you. For example, losing your job or becoming injured and not being able to work would be a major burden for most people. Think about your own circumstances. What could happen in your life that you would consider a financial crisis? Are you prepared if this were to happen?

Here's an article that discusses some of the ways that you can prepare yourself for the next financial crisis. **https://finance.yahoo.com/news/millennials-can-prepare-next-financial-crisis-151728542.html**

*

One of the best ways to deal with anxiety about finances is to have a goal-based plan and stick with it. Your goals are personal and may differ from your friends and that's ok. For example, you may have a five- year plan, with your goals being to pay off your debts and save up for a car. Your friend may have a plan to save up for a down payment on a home and increase their retirement savings. Regardless of what your goals are, creating a plan and sticking with it will help you feel more confident about your finances.

*

The "2017 Millennial Survey: Millennials, Money, and the Happiness Factor" conducted by Wells Fargo revealed some interesting data about how Millennials feel about their finances. Feeling financially secure was important to 98% of those surveyed. So what does financial security look like? There is not one size fits all for the definition of financial security. Perhaps for some it might be a steady job, with consistent income. For others it might be the ability to move upwards within a company, and yet for some it might mean having $50,000 sitting in the bank. For others, it might mean having their student debt paid off (or at least a good plan to do so!).

Of course we all want to feel financially secure, but for each of us it may mean something different. What does financial security look like to you?

*

A recent survey by Student Loan Hero showed that professionals early in their careers stress the most about:

1. Having too much debt
2. Their inability to afford rent and other necessities
3. Difficulty managing a budget.

What about you? What money challenges cause you the most stress? What money gremlins are in your life?

*

In yet another survey of Millennials done by Acorns, not all Millennials have the same financial concerns. 41% of survey respondents ages 24-35 feel they won't be financially secure enough to retire until they are older than 65 years old. While only 5% of younger respondents (ages 18-23) are actively investing. Also, 70% of respondents said they felt their high school education did not prepare them to manage their finances and 39% feel anxious about their financial future.

Finally, 50% of Millennials surveyed said they are not sure about how to invest, but do feel it is important to learn. Take some time to read a few books about investing and you'll ease your anxiety by gaining some knowledge. We recommend "*I Will Teach You to Be Rich*" by Ramit Sethi, and "*Ditch the Guesswork: Creating Reliable ROI for Time-Starved Investors*" by Steve Juetten, CFP® (and the Principal of our company).

Chelsea Says:

Over the last few years, while taking many financial planning courses, I've been forced to confront my own personal financial situation (over and over). Sometimes when I think about my finances, I feel good about the choices I've made. Other times, I look at my finances and feel worried and anxious that I'm not on track or that I'm not doing enough. What I have come to learn is that I cannot compare myself to others. My situation is unique to me and my family. The best way for me to judge my financial situation is by determining whether or not I am putting in the effort to achieve the goals that are important to me.

When I start to irrationally worry myself (which happens more often than I'd like), I try to center my thoughts on what I've done right in the past, and also remind myself that I'm still working towards my goals in the future. Would I like to have my children's college savings completely funded right now? Sure. But I'm ok with where I'm at now because I know I'm doing my best to keep steering my family in the right direction

Additional Resources

We've all been concerned about our finances at one point or another. And sometimes that anxiety from worrying can get to be overwhelming. Here's a great article that gives some tips on things you can do to ease your anxiety about your personal finances.
http://www.moneycrashers.com/financial-anxiety-stressed-about-money/

MAIL BAG QUESTIONS

Note: we receive questions from friends, emails from clients and when we do presentations to groups of early career professionals. We decided to keep a list and answer them in a separate section and rather than call this section "Miscellaneous" or something boring like that, we call this our "Mail Bag".

*

How much house can I afford?

Ideally your home payment, whether it's rent or a mortgage, should be around 33% of your take home pay. Banks may approve you for a mortgage with a monthly payment greater than 33% of your take home pay, but that does not mean that you have to take the maximum of what you are approved for. You can use the mortgage calculator at **www.bankrate.com/calculators.aspx** to give you an idea of what your monthly payments might look like.

*

How much do I need to retire?

It depends on when you want to retire. Start by saving at least 10% of your gross income. If you're in your 20's or 30's, as you receive pay raises and as you get older, increase the amount you save to 15%. If the increase in savings is done slowly and as you increase your pay, you shouldn't notice it affecting your lifestyle.

The total amount you need to retire depends on what you see yourself doing on a daily basis during retirement. It depends on where you plan to live and what you plan to do. The amount an individual needs in order to retire is completely unique to that person. That's why it's important to consult with a financial planner about your situation. They should help talk you through all the important considerations and help you determine the appropriate amount of money you will need in order to retire and live the life you want to live during retirement. **http://www.investopedia.com/articles/financial-advisors/122815/how-much-millennials-should-save-retire-comfortably.asp**

*

What can I invest in that will be safe but pay high returns?

The return of an investment is tied to the investment's riskiness. The greater the risk, the greater the potential return. The less risk, the less the return. Therefore, there is no investment that will be safe and pay high returns. Or, as Steve likes to say, *"There's no such thing as a free lunch."*

*

How much life insurance do I need? Or do I need any?

Life insurance is a way to protect against income interruption. If you are single and have kids, a life insurance policy on you will provide your children's caretakers with money they can use to take care of them in the event of your passing. This insurance money is essentially replacing what you would have been providing for them, had you still been alive. The same goes for married couples, especially if one is the majority breadwinner.

There are two basic types of life insurance:

1. Term insurance lasts for a specific number of years and provides a death benefit during that

period as long as the premiums are paid. Most people only need this type of life insurance.

2. Whole life insurance provides a death benefit and accumulates value; there are many variations to whole life insurance including universal life. Most people don't need this type of coverage.

Here's a good article that discusses life insurance types:

www.nerdwallet.com/blog/insurance/types-of-life-insurance/

The amount of life insurance you may need depends on what you expect that money to go towards. If you're married and both work, you may only choose to have enough life insurance to cover your debts. This means that the surviving spouse would continue working, but not have to worry about making the mortgage or car payment. Or, if you're in a family where there is only one income, you may want to choose the amount of insurance that would cover the equivalent of a lifetime of earnings of the breadwinner.

You can use a life insurance calculator at one of these websites to give you an idea of the amount of life insurance you might need.

Visit **www.lifehappens.org** or **www.bankrate.com** for these calculators.

*

Can I put money in a Roth IRA?

Maybe. If you have earned income or you have a spouse who has earned income, you may be able to contribute to a Roth IRA. The maximum you can contribute to a Roth IRA is $5,500 per year if you're under 50 years old. The amount you can contribute decreases if you are married and jointly have modified adjusted gross income (MAGI) of more than $186,000 per year, or if you are single and make more than $118,000 per year, with no contributions allowed if your income is above $196,000 for married couples or $133,000 for singles. And you are allowed to contribute to a Roth IRA even if you also participate in your employer sponsored retirement plan, assuming your income is less than the amounts outlined above. (Note: remember these are the limits and rules as of 2018. The IRS often changes these so be sure to check with a qualified tax expert before investing in a Roth IRA or Traditional IRA.)

*

Sometimes I'm invited by friends out to dinner or brunch and found myself torn between saying yes because I want to hang out with my friends, but I also want to say no because I know that it's not the best choice for me financially. Any suggestions?

You aren't alone. We get this question pretty often. First, don't be afraid to say "no." Good friends will understand. Then, make suggestions for activities that don't cost money, like hiking. I'm willing to bet most of your friends would appreciate a low-cost activity once in a while. Check out this article on how FOMO (Fear of Missing Out) is leading Millennials into debt.
https://www.bustle.com/p/millennials-are-going-into-debt-to-avoid-fomo-a-new-survey-says-its-a-pretty-serious-issue-8707616

*

Sometimes the stock market goes way down and it makes me nervous. Shouldn't I just take my money out at times like this and wait for the stock market to stop acting so crazy?

In Burton Malkiel's book "**A Random Walk Down Wall Street**" he notes that if you had invested $1 in the Dow Jones Industrial Average (an index of 30 major U.S. stocks) in 1900, by the start of 2013 it would have grown to $290. If you had missed out on only the best five days of each year during that time period, that same $1 would have been worth less than a penny in 2013.

This just goes to show that being out of the market for even just a few days each year can have a dramatic impact on your returns. That's why when investing in the stock market, you've got to be in it for the long-run and not try to time when to get in or out of your investments. It's like planting a tree and watching it grow – you wouldn't run out and pull it up every time it rains or snows or the wind blows hard, would you?

*

How much cash should we have on hand for emergencies?

We recommend you have three to six months' worth of living expenses saved for emergencies. Living expenses included in this calculation include rent/mortgage, any debt payments, utility bills, grocery expenses, and any other expenses that are considered necessities. Imagine if you were to lose your job, you'd probably try to cut back on eating at restaurants or taking vacations. These are not necessities and shouldn't be included in your living expenses calculation. If your income varies from paycheck to paycheck, we'd suggest having closer to six months of expenses. If you're in a stable job with a steady income, you may be okay with closer to three months of expenses at hand.

*

What's going to happen to the stock market?

No one can predict what will happen to the investment markets. You may hear people say that based on trends and analysis that the stock market is supposed to fall, or that whenever XYZ happens the stock market goes up. But no one can actually predict what will happen. With that said, history shows that the stock market has gone up over long periods of time with intermittent downturns that test us all. The best approach is build a diversified portfolio as a long-term investing tool, make choices for investing based on your personal situation and goals and stick with it.

*

Is our house an investment?

Your house is an **asset**. You pay to live there each month, and when you decide you do not want to live there anymore, you can sell it and receive some of that money back, perhaps even more than you paid. Yet as most of us know, the amount that you could receive when selling your house can fluctuate. Therefore a home should not be seen as a way to make a profit but as a place to enjoy life and build memories.

*

I hear a lot about Bitcoin. Should I invest in it or is it too late?

First, Bitcoin is not an "investment" – it's a gamble like playing roulette at the casino. Sure, some people win big at the roulette table, but most don't. Let us explain.

Bitcoin is a decentralized digital currency that operates as a blockchain. A blockchain is a type of live distributed ledger; think of it as Google Sheets where updates (or transactions) occur in real-time. These transactions are public, but the identities behind the transactions can be anonymous

Blockchain currencies (for ease of reading we'll use Bitcoin) disrupts traditional middleman approach, such as centralized banks and payment processing companies, because you send and receive Bitcoins through a digital wallet. Because Bitcoin is a distributed ledger, funds you send will be recorded as coming from your wallet and going to another wallet.

Unlike a traditional bank account, there are no regulations for Bitcoin, meaning your digital wallet can be anonymous. Bitcoin is currently* outside of the Securities and Exchange Commission's (SEC) oversight. However, this also means no refunds and little to no accountability!!

We don't consider Bitcoin an investment like stock and bonds because it has no underlying value. John Bogle, the founder of the investment company Vanguard, stated, "Bitcoin has no underlying rate of return -- bonds have an interest coupon, stocks have earnings and dividends. There is nothing to support Bitcoin except the *hope* that you will sell it to someone for more than you paid for it." Sounds like a classic investment scam to us; a form of musical chairs or the greater fool model.

The only return you can earn from holding Bitcoin is its price appreciation and that is very un-certain (we'll explain this more below). Why is this an issue? Well, it's hard to plan for your financial future if your investment product has no underlying value associated with it. What do we mean by that? Stocks and bonds have a long track record of growth, volatility and returns that we can use to create a financial plan, whereas Bitcoin lacks earnings, distributions or a long-term history. In financial planning terms, Bitcoin lacks a high probability.

Additionally, there are many risks in the Bitcoin market:

1. **Congestion risk**: Because Bitcoin is a distributed ledger that records all transactions, as more people join the exchange, and the number of desired transactions increase, the system slows down as orders line up. This means you could put in an order in to send, sell or buy at a certain price, only to watch and wait until it's your turn and find that the price has changed. Additionally, the fee paid to the miners who record and verify transactions increases as demand increases (capitalism at work) thus decreasing the value of your Bitcoin.

2. **Regulation risk**: Just because the SEC doesn't currently consider Bitcoin a security, doesn't mean they won't start regulating it. If they do start, that could mean an exodus of people who want an unregulated market, or added costs for compliance and transactions. Additionally, governments around the world have been reviewing their laws surrounding Bitcoin and may regulate it in unforeseen ways, or outright ban its use.

3. **Taxation risk**: Unlike currency, Bitcoins held as a capital asset are taxed as property. But Bitcoins paid for goods and services are taxed as regular income. You must keep detailed records of all your Bitcoin transactions and report any gains through transactions. Failure to do so can result in heavy penalties, including jail time! Just because the currency is digital, and your wallet is anonymous, doesn't mean you can ignore the IRS.*

4. **Market Manipulation**: Because of low volume (compared to regular currencies and traditional investments), Bitcoin and other blockchain currencies are susceptible to pump and dump and market manipulation. Additionally, because it is an unregulated industry, you can't complete

due diligence before exchanging your money for Bitcoins. And if you are victim of fraud (for example, paying for a good or service with Bitcoins) there is little to no recourse! Buyer Beware!

5. **New Entries & Forks**: While there are a few coins that dominate the market, new entries seem to be popping up daily. **There are currently over 900 varieties of cryptocurriencies.** The risk with Bitcoin, like with many products, is that a new one becomes more popular. Remember what happened to the Blackberry mobile phone? Once it was the standard for mobile phones, but then the iPhone and Android phones came on to the market and the Blackberry became irrelevant. With Bitcoin, a large risk is the possibility that a new product comes to market backed by a large institution or government that people feel safer using and that becomes the standard, making Bitcoin like the Blackberry (irrelevant).

"Forks" are programmed splits within the currency that are similar to planned obsolesce. Forks create a situation where you have to decide if you want to stay with the outdated coin, or adopt the new version. Bitcoin has already had two since its founding in 2009 and a third in

November 2017 was abruptly called off due to concerns over splitting the currency.

6. **Exchange Rate Risk**: If we think of Bitcoin as a currency, then the risk is that the value of it in relation to the dollar goes down after you purchase it. It's hard (impossible) to predict which direction the price of Bitcoins will go, so keep that in mind if you are looking at purchasing some.

Finally, we want to comment on the phenomenon called Fear of Missing Out (FOMO). Whenever there is a lot of media attention on a product, some people fear getting left out (FOMO). We see it all the time around us: concert tickets to the hottest new performer, tickets to Hamilton the musical, the latest Tesla car, or house flipping in 2007. Whenever there is perceived scarcity of a product or experience, and high demand, some people will be worried that they will somehow be worse off because they are not "in the game." We see some of this behavior with Bitcoin.

All investing carries risk and blockchain currencies introduce new risks that haven't been evaluated or tested because the industry is still new and largely unregulated. Thus, if you feel you must be "in the game" of cryptocurrency, first examine why you are interested.

Is it because you think it's a good investment or do you enjoy gambling or is it FOMO? If you think blockchain is an idea whose time has come, consider focusing on the companies in the blockchain industry. Who is adopting the technology behind Bitcoin? Will it make their business more profitable? Efficient? Above all else, it's important to remember the five rules of investing.

- Risk and return are related

- Diversification improves returns

- No one can predict the future

- Passive beats active

- Costs matter

*Caveat: The regulatory environment is playing catch-up with Bitcoin. In a ruling in late November 2017, a federal court judge ordered San Francisco-based Coinbase to comply with a summons that requires it to identify 14,355 accounts, which have accounted for nearly 9 million Bitcoin transactions, to the IRS. The SEC has also hinted at regulating Bitcoin as a security and governments outside the U.S. are considering their own regulations.

ABOUT THE FINANCIAL FOUNDATIONS PROGRAM

The Financial Foundations Program was started by **Juetten Personal Financial Planning LLC** in 2017 as a way for early career professionals to affordably obtain high quality fee-only financial planning. Early career professionals face unique challenges such as high housing costs, student loans and a dynamic workforce. Our focus is on your goals and how we can empower you to make smart money decisions. We act as fiduciaries for our clients; this means we don't sell any products or receive commissions, and we always act in your best interests.

We're more than money managers. We like to travel, explore the great Northwest and be with family. We all have a sense of pride in what we do and probably spend too much time talking finance with those around us.

The Financial Foundations Program was created to serve early career professionals who are in general excluded from more traditional financial planning services either due to costs, small amount of assets or because the firms do not specialize in working with early career professionals.

We believe that advice should be affordable, free from conflicts of interest and that your needs are always front and center. In 2017, the **Financial Foundations Program** was a finalist in the Bellevue Chamber of Commerce annual contest in the "Most Innovative Company" category.

ABOUT THE AUTHORS

Kyle Wilke, CFP®

Kyle started his path on financial planning working with refugees and immigrants where he provided financial literacy and small business consulting. He's a Seattle native although he has spent a considerable amount of time in Thailand as a child. He completed his BA in international studies from the Jackson School for International Studies at the University of Washington. He is an enthusiastic educator and loves to guide people in an approachable manner. He serves clients in the tech, engineering and bio-medical sectors but is familiar with nonprofit and educator areas as well. Kyle is a new Dad and dog owner. In his spare time, you can find him babysitting, running with the dog, on a sports field, traveling or in the kitchen baking a pie. You can reach him at **kyle@finpath.com**.

Chelsea Hodl, MBA

Chelsea Hodl became interested in personal finance when she saw how it was affecting people in her family.

She received her Bachelor's in Business Administration from the University of San Diego and decided to return back to school to pursue her Master's degree. She received her MBA in Financial Planning from California Lutheran University in 2014. She has lived on both the East Coast and West Coast, but settled down in her hometown of Spokane where she and her husband are raising their two boys. She keeps busy with her kids' sports activities, and when she does have some free time she enjoys scrapbooking and crafting and doing volunteer work. You can reach her at **Chelsea@finpath.com**.

Steve Juetten, CFP®

Since 2002, busy career professionals have trusted CERTIFIED FINANCIAL PLANNER™ Professional Steve for personal financial guidance. All are treated to the same simple, respectful and direct counsel that comes from being raised in the Midwest and loving what he does. Steve helps clients identify where they want to go in their lives, evaluate where they stand now from a financial perspective and help them create and follow the financial steps that guide them to achieve their goals.

He is a fee-only financial adviser and is a fiduciary for his clients. "Fee-only" means that Steve does not sell any products (other than an occasional book he writes!) or take commissions so clients can trust his objective, independent advice and counsel. As a fiduciary, Steve is legally required to put his clients' best interest ahead of his own, avoiding conflicts of interest and operating with fee transparency.

Steve has been a featured expert on Bankrate.com, PBS.com, Forbes.com, MSNMoney.com, FOXBusiness.com, and the *Puget Sound Business Journal*. His clients seem to like what he does to help them. *Seattle Magazine* has named Steve a FIVE STAR WEALTH MANAGER for five years in a row.

Steve is the Managing Member and Principal of Juetten Personal Financial Planning, LLC, a Registered Investment Adivsor firm located in Bellevue, Washington (www.finpath.com). He leads a small team of dedicated professionals committed to helping their clients achieve their goals through careful application of a 360° financial planning and wealth management system. You can reach him at **steve@finpath.com**.

HAVE A QUESTION FOR US?

We have answers! There are several ways we can help you:

1. Visit our website at **www.takecareofyourmoney.com** to learn more about how we can be of service.
2. **Visit our Facebook page** where we post articles and videos very often.
3. Take our financial wellness quiz at **www.fwquiz.com** and get a personalized score on your financial well-being.
4. Email either Kyle (**kyle@finpath.com**) or Chelsea (**Chelsea@finpath.com**) for a free Get Acquainted session where you can explore your issues and challenges with a fee-only advisor, and we can discuss how we might be able to assist you.
5. Book Kyle to speak at your professional group or networking event. He loves to present personal financial topics live and answer questions.

Make Smart Money Moves!

Get on track and stay on track early in your career. You'll have more confidence, avoid mistakes, make the most of your resources and create a life you love.